THE GREATER GOOD WORKBOOK

A unique step-by-step, holistic a
social entrepreneurship, based on the aw

THE GREATER GOOD

Social Entrepreneurship for Everyday People Who Want to Change the World

MADELEINE SHAW

Ideal for instructors using *The Greater Good* as course material OR for individual use

A companion guide to *The Greater Good* that includes reading guide, learning objectives, activities, supplemental resources and discussion questions

The Greater Good Workbook
Published by Madeleine Shaw
Vancouver, BC, Canada.

For information regarding this publication, email m@greatergood.work

SHAW, MADELEINE, Author
THE GREATER GOOD WORKBOOK
MADELEINE SHAW

Design: Hayley Schmidt
Cover design and cover illustration: Morgan Krehbiel

ISBN: 978-1-7381747-0-6 (paperback)

This book is printed in the United States of America.

TABLE OF CONTENTS

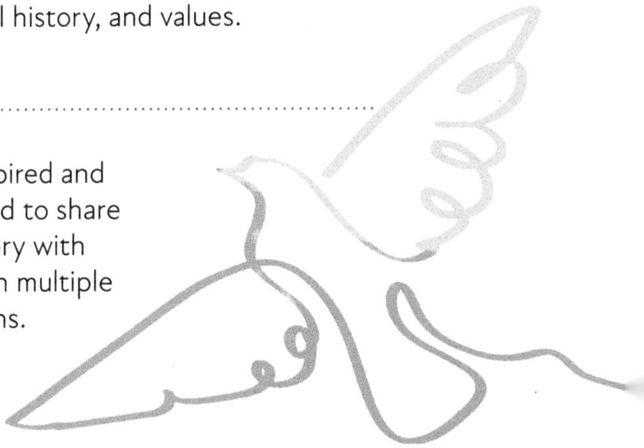

TABLE OF CONTENTS

INTRODUCTION

Learning Outcome

Develop a clear understanding of the concept of social entrepreneurship in terms of what it is, who it applies to, and what is needed to put it into action.

Learning notes

"Which brings me to you, wonderful everyday person who wants to change the world. Let's do this together. My feeling is that when we include everyone, especially those who have been marginalized or underrepresented, we start to see the most healing, innovative, and game-changing ideas emerge. It's an opportunity to redefine ourselves and what matters to us in order to move into a new era of inclusion, creativity, and values-driven entrepreneurial practices."

Learning Materials

Book:

- *The Greater Good* Introduction

This section is an empowering message from the author about her motivation for writing the book: the state of the world and how we need everyone–especially those who may not yet identify as changemakers–to contribute their ideas, creativity and life experience to making the world a better place.

Madeleine Shaw's website:

- Social entrepreneurship *https://madeleineshaw.ca/social-entrepreneurship/*

Videos:

- Grow Ensemble: What is Social Entrepreneurship (7:27) *https://www.youtube.com/watch?v=5U7opm_8DNk*
- Meet Aisle (4:25) *https://vimeo.com/395043346*
- The G Day Movement (2:21) *https://www.youtube.com/watch?v=LeLmDfZ046E&t=3s*
- *The Greater Good* (1:55) *https://www.youtube.com/watch?v=Cf_7AuhGL4c*
- What is Nestworks (3:59) *https://www.youtube.com/watch?v=h_Jeu-sPOxU*

Key Terms and Definitions

Social entrepreneur

Someone who initiates a project or venture to create positive social or environmental change, at any scale.

Social enterprise

A project or venture, either for- or non-profit, that has positive social or environmental impact as its primary guiding force.

Questions for Discussion

- Who is Madeleine Shaw?
- Who are social entrepreneurs?
- What is social entrepreneurship?
- Why is social entrepreneurship important in these disrupted times?

Additional Resources

Media:

- Grow Ensemble is a community built to raise awareness and inspire meaningful action around the world's most important issues: *https://growensemble.com*

Blogpost:

- How to Become a Social Entrepreneur with Madeleine Shaw: *https://growensemble.com/how-to-become-a-social-entrepreneur/*

Video:

- *Not Business as Usual* (1:01:34) *https://www.youtube.com/watch?v=p_TCDS-V6Aw&feature=youtu.be*
    - *Not Business As Usual* is a provocative look at capitalism and its unintended price of success. The film tracks the changing landscape of business with the rising tide of conscious capitalism through the stories of local entrepreneurs who have found innovative ways to bring humanity back into business.
- *The Social Shift*, A Documentary on Business for the Common Good *https://www.thesocialshift.ca/*

ACTIVITY I.1:

WHAT IS YOUR DEFINITION OF AN ENTREPRENEUR?

Learning Materials

Book:

- *The Greater Good* - Introduction

Madeleine Shaw's website:

- Social entrepreneurship *https://madeleineshaw.ca/social-entrepreneurship/*

Videos:

- Grow Ensemble: What is Social Entrepreneurship (7:27) *https://www.youtube.com/watch?v=5U7opm_8DNk*

Podcast:

- In With the New podcast: Social Entrepreneurship, Sustainability, and Reusable Menstrual Products *https://podcasts.apple.com/us/podcast/social-entrepreneurship-sustainability-and-reusableid1668024207?i=1000596934013*

Format

Small group discussion or self-reflection.

Prior to reading the book introduction or watching the video, consider the following questions:

- What was your definition of an entrepreneur?
- When you thought about the term entrepreneur, who came to mind? What images, concepts, or ideas came to mind?
- Had you heard of the term social entrepreneur before? What did you think that it meant?
- Can you think of any examples of people or businesses that you feel would be social entrepreneurs given your definition?

After reading the book introduction or watching the video, consider the following questions:

- Did your definitions of entrepreneur and social entrepreneur change?
- Did the people, businesses, images, concepts, or ideas that come to mind change? Why or why not?
- Has this changed how you see the possibility of yourself as an entrepreneur?

ACTIVITY I.1 - NOTES

ACTIVITY 1.2:

CHANGING THE WORLD

Learning Materials

Videos:

Videos highlighting Madeleine Shaw's social entrepreneur ventures

- Meet Aisle (4:25) *https://vimeo.com/395043346*
- The G Day Movement (2:21) *https://www.youtube.com/watch?v=LeLmDfZ046E&t=3s*
- *The Greater Good* (1:55) *https://www.youtube.com/watch?v=Cf_7AuhGL4c*
- What is Nestworks (3:59) *https://www.youtube.com/watch?v=h_Jeu-sPOxU*

Format

- **Option A:** Choose one (or more) videos and describe how it illustrates the concept of social entrepreneurship.
- **Option B:** Assign a video to a small group to describe how it illustrates the concept of social entrepreneurship. Have the small group share their insights with the larger group.

ACTIVITY 1.2 - NOTES

"A forest of seemingly separate trees has vast networks of roots connecting them from beneath."

Learning Outcome

Understand how social entrepreneurship can create much needed change in the world.

Learning Notes

- **Importance of lesson**
- **Important considerations for this lesson**

"We find ourselves defining our projects or brands based on how we measure up to these other offerings, as opposed to looking within and showcasing our unique light and story as well as those we seek to serve."

"I believe our economic systems can evolve and that the practice of business, and capitalism itself have the potential to move from an extractive, transactional form into one that is regenerative and relational."

Learning Materials

Book:

- *The Greater Good* - Chapter 1: Everyday People Doing Extraordinary Things
- An overview of social entrepreneurship and spotlights of inspiring examples.

Videos:

- How to Be a Social Entrepreneur Video Course: Episode 1:
  Part 1 - The Power of Everyday People (5:08) *https://www.youtube. com/watch?v=U85WmXecDQM*
- Madeleine Shaw's website: Social entrepreneur profiles *https://madeleineshaw.ca/profiles/*
- Grow Ensemble Blogpost: 50 Social Entrepreneurs Changing the World *https://growensemble.com/social-entrepreneurs/*

TED Talks:

- Dr. Suzanne Simard: "How trees talk to each other"
- Professor of Forest Ecology at the University of British Columbia *https://www.ted.com/talks/suzanne_simard_how_trees_talk_to_each_other?language=en* (18:10)
- "A forest is much more than what you see," says ecologist Suzanne Simard. Her 30 years of research in Canadian forests have led to an astounding discovery—trees talk, often and over vast distances. Learn more about the harmonious yet complicated social lives of trees and prepare to see the natural world with new eyes."
- Kate Raworth: "A healthy economy should be designed to thrive, not grow"
- Economist, Senior Associate at Oxford University, Professor of Practice at Amsterdam University of Applied Sciences *https://www.ted.com/talks/kate_raworth_a_healthy_economy_should_be_designed_to_thrive_not_grow?language=en* (15:44)
- What would a sustainable, universally beneficial economy look like? "Like a doughnut," says Oxford economist Kate Raworth. In a stellar, eye-opening talk, she explains how we can move countries out of the hole—where people are falling short on life's essentials—and create regenerative, distributive economies that work within the planet's ecological limits.

Key Terms and Definitions

Biomimicry

The adaptation of natural systems to address complex human problems.

Collaboration

Working with others to produce or create something.

Competition

The act or process of trying to get or win something others are also trying to get or win.

Everyday people

Most of us; a truly diverse range of people from all walks of life.

Nestworks supporters and board members, 2020

Radical generosity

An open ended belief system in terms of what is available to us, as opposed to the assumption that whatever we seek to obtain needs to be wrestled away from someone else, and that resources overall—whether physical, imaginative, or intellectual—are limited.

Questions for discussion

- What does 'collaboration is the new competition' mean?
- What are some examples of ways that social entrepreneurs are different from their traditional colleagues?

Additional Resources

Books:

- *Finding the Mother Tree: Discovering the Wisdom of the Forest* by Suzanne Simard https://suzannesimard.com/finding-the-mother-tree-book/
- *Doughnut Economics: 7 Ways to Think Like a 21st Century Economist* by Kate Raworth https://www.amazon.com/Doughnut-Economics-Seven-21st-Century-Economist/dp/1603586741/
- *It's About Damn Time: How to Turn Being Underestimated into Your Greatest Advantage* by Arlan Hamilton https://www.goodreads.com/book/show/49646727-it-s-about-damn-time

CHAPTER 1 - ACTIVITIES

ACTIVITY 1.1:

COLLABORATION IS THE NEW COMPETITION

Learning Materials

Book:

- *The Greater Good* - Chapter 1

TED Talks:

- Suzanne Simard: "How Trees Talk To Each Other" *https://www.ted.com/talks/suzanne_simard_how_trees_talk_to_each_other?language=en* (18:10)
- Kate Raworth: "A healthy economy should be designed to thrive, not grow" *https://www.ted.com/talks/kate_raworth_a_healthy_economy_should_be_designed_to_thrive_not_grow?language=en* (15:44)

Format

Self-reflection with option for small group sharing and discussion.

The book *The Greater Good* isn't just about business and it isn't just about human organizations. It is about the natural world. Social entrepreneurship involves taking our cues from nature and working with nature. Consider the concept of biomimicry - the adaptation of natural systems to address complex human problems. For example, a forest of seemingly separate trees has vast networks of roots connecting them from beneath. In droughts and other times of stress, the root network transmits information and nutrients between the trees and can even bind together to physically support them during storms. This truly highlights the concept of "collaboration over competition".

- How have you imagined business as an inherently competitive activity before and after watching and thinking about the ideas discussed?
- Does business need to be competitive? What are the downsides of that? What if it could be different?
- What does the phrase "collaboration is the new competition" mean to you?
- What are your thoughts on the concept of biomimicry and how the adaptation of natural systems can address complex human problems?

ACTIVITY 1.1 - NOTES

ACTIVITY 1.2:

EVERYDAY PEOPLE CHANGING THE WORLD

Learning Materials

Book:

- *The Greater Good* - Chapter 1

Video:

- How to Be a Social Entrepreneur Video Course: Episode 1: Part 1 - The Power of Everyday People (5:08) *https://www.youtube.com/watch?v=U85WmXecDQM*

Madeleine Shaw's website:

- Social entrepreneur profiles *https://madeleineshaw.ca/profiles/*

Grow Ensemble Blogpost

- 50 Social Entrepreneurs Changing the World *https://growensemble.com/social-entrepreneurs/*

Format

Small group discussion or self-reflection.

Choose at least 2 social entrepreneurs profiled in the learning materials:

- What are their ventures?
- What is the change they are seeking to create?
- What do you notice about the social entrepreneurs that have been profiled?
- How are these social entrepreneurs different from their traditional colleagues?
- What resonated and stood out for you?
- Which did you want to explore further and learn more about? Why?
- How are the entrepreneurs that you chose examples of everyday people changing the world?
- Do you know someone who fits this profile?

ACTIVITY 1.2 - NOTES

Learning Outcome

Recognize the value of individual life experience, intuition, imagination, possibilities, and creative thought as opposed to traditional business skills.

Learning Notes

- **Importance of lesson**
- **Important considerations for this lesson**

"If you were looking to make the world a better place, folks who have been oppressed or excluded by traditional power systems would have fresh ideas for something different, better, and more humane."

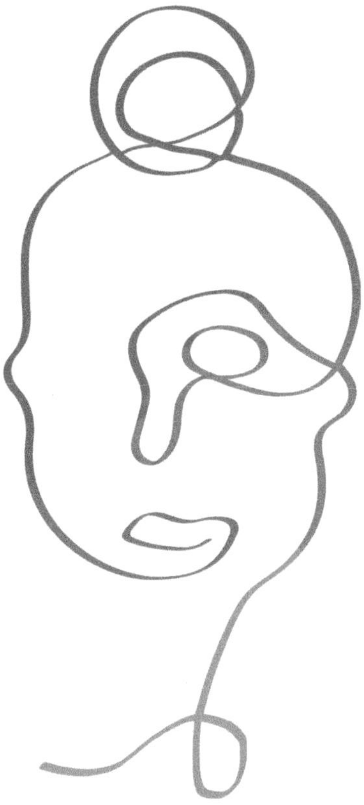

Learning Materials

Book:

- *The Greater Good* - Chapter 2: Soul Traits of Social Entrepreneurs

The characteristics successful social entrepreneurs and changemakers share, such as displaying grit in the face of challenge, a willingness to transform and embracing a collaborative leadership style.

Key Terms and Definitions

Soul Traits

Characteristics of social entrepreneurs.

Questions for discussion

- What relationships can you see between entrepreneurs' life journeys and their ventures?
- How do these personal experiences shape and change how they approach their ventures?

CHAPTER 2 - ACTIVITIES

ACTIVITY 2.1:

SOUL TRAITS OF SOCIAL ENTREPRENEURS

Learning Materials

Book:

- *The Greater Good* - Chapter 2

Format

Small group discussion or personal reflection.

In *The Greater Good*, Madeleine Shaw shares the key 'soul traits' of social entrepreneurs.

These include:

- **Coloring outside the lines** - Generating creative, unique, innovative ideas and organizational models.
- **True grit** - Having the patience, tenacity, and determination to persist, often in the face of immense challenges.
- **Making lemonade** - Using personal trauma/adversity as creative fuel.
- **Gifts from the margins** - Using unique perspectives brought about by being outside the dominant culture to inspire new ideas and insights.
- **Stronger together** - Asking for help, working collaboratively, and building community.
- **Impact is the new black** - Having impact is not just a nice-to-have: it's the entire rationale, and an immense source of inspiration, energy, creativity, and drive.
- **Impact is also the new currency** - Being motivated by big impact versus big financial scale.
- **Willingness to transform** - Being willing to change key self-perceptions in order to realize your vision.
- **Honoring your calling** - Listening to and acting on persistent inner voices or recurring patterns to feel like they are 'calling you'.
- **Dancing with the demons** - Making peace with your demons (e.g. imposter syndrome, fear of failure, profound self-doubt), rather than crushing them, in order to move forward.

Consider how these soul traits land for you. Do you identify with any of them? Which ones and why? Did they inspire more traits to add to this list? If so, what are they?

ACTIVITY 2.1 - NOTES

ACTIVITY 2.2:

CREATE YOUR OWN BUSINESS ACRONYM

Learning Materials

Book:

- *The Greater Good* - Chapter 2

Format

Individual or small group exercise.

Try on the soul trait of 'coloring outside of the lines' for yourself! Social entrepreneurs are by definition "redefiners" in that they inherently question the accepted purpose of business-as-usual capitalism by putting the "social" part first. These folks go even further, though, coming up with their own definitions of goals, scale, profits, success, and more.

There are many existing acronyms in the world of business. These are traditionally accepted wisdom. For example:

- **TEAM** = Together Everyone Achieves More
- **ROI** = Return on Investment
- **BHAG** = Big Hairy Audacious Goal

Somebody made these up and you can come up with the latest business buzz worthy acronym if you want to as well!

Generate your own meaning for or reframe an existing acronym

For example:

- **BHAG** traditionally stands for "big, hairy, audacious goal".
    - Madeleine prefers "beautiful, healthy, achievable, generative" as her personal success metric.
- **VUCA** (volatile, uncertain, complex, ambiguous) is a post-Cold War US Army term that was coined to describe the worldview of the day and has regained popularity in common business vernacular in recent years. For a presentation that Madeleine and Suzanne Siemens did for an audience of women entrepreneur clients of a major Canadian bank in Calgary, they, instead, came up with:
- **CODE:** Colorful, Opportunity-rich, Diverse, Evolving

Make up your own acronym that means something for you personally. How does it make you feel, to see that you are capable of doing this?

ACTIVITY 2.2 - NOTES

CHAPTER 3 | FINDING YOUR WHY

Learning Outcome

Develop greater clarity and insight into the personal values that shape and underlie the change that we want to create in the world.

Learning Notes

- **Importance of lesson**
- **Important considerations for this lesson**

"The types of insights that we are looking for can show up at any time, not just when we are intentionally seeking them."

Learning Materials

Book:

- *The Greater Good* - Chapter 3: Finding Your Why

Finding inspiration by looking at personal history and being your own "personal detective," with prompts for readers and examples from established changemakers.

Collection of personally resonant objects, photographs, and mementos.

Notebook, file, or corkboard to gather materials and ideas in one place.

Key Terms and Definitions

Personal Story

A personal narrative which focuses on identity, growth, reflections, and life-lessons.

Values

A set of principles or beliefs that consciously or unconsciously guide your life choices and pursuits.

Questions for discussion

- What are creative ways that can be used to develop a deeper understanding of our values and what matters to us?

Additional Resources

Podcast:

- Below the Radar (Simon Fraser University) Episode 15: A Feminist Career with Madeleine Shaw (36:18) - Simon Fraser University (Podcast) *https://www.sfu.ca/vancity-office-community-engagement/below-the-radar-podcast/episodes/15-madeleine-shaw.html*

CHAPTER 3 - ACTIVITIES

ACTIVITY 3.1:

SELF-REFLECTION WARM-UP

Learning Materials

Book:

- *The Greater Good* - Chapter 3
- Collection of personally resonant objects, photographs, and mementos

Format

Individual exercise with option to share in a group setting.

- Assemble a collection of personally resonant objects, photographs, and mementos
- Document your thoughts during this process.
  - You could use large sticky notes with colorful markers, an online virtual whiteboard tool such as Miro, or whatever works for you!
  - You may want to listen to music or to journal to help with the flow of ideas as you gather your items.
- Arrange these items on a table or floor space and consider each one.
- Write down:
  - Where did it come from?
  - Why is it significant to you?
  - Did someone give it to you, or did you choose it?
  - What is its story and why does that story mean enough to you that you keep this object in your home?
  - Are there any themes or patterns that arise?
  - Any particular memories or feelings that surface?

ACTIVITY 3.1 - NOTES

ACTIVITY 3.2:

PERSONAL STORY MAPPING

Learning Materials

Book:

- *The Greater Good* - Chapter 3

Format

Individual exercise with option to share in a group setting.

Address one or more of the following to look more closely at your personal history. Record your thoughts and ideas using words, pictures or drawings, or a combination of both.

- Do a bullet point inventory or map of your life's journey. What have the most impactful experiences been?
- Create an autobiography
- How have you defined yourself in the past? Who do you see yourself as now? How do you see yourself in an ideal future?
- What are things you love? Hate? Feel deeply curious about?
- What are your resources?
- What are your constraints?

ACTIVITY 3.2 - NOTES

Madeleine and her Aisle co-founder Suzanne Siemens at work.

ACTIVITY 3.3:

VALUES EXERCISE

Learning Materials

- *The Greater Good* - Chapter 3
- Know Your Values cards (optional). Available via *leadershipcollaboratory.com*

Format

Individual exercise with option to share in a group setting.

Looking at your values is another good way to point your compass toward the kernel of an idea that may be meaningful. The goal for this exercise is to come up with a list of words or phrases that represent your values as well as noticing your physical and emotional responses.

Example: Madeleine's principles

1. Step up
2. Stay open
3. Let it flow
4. Do the thing
5. Make space
6. Feel everything
7. Nurture
8. Be strong
9. Be awesome

Example: Design firm IDEO

1. Talk less, do more
2. Make others successful
3. Learn from failure
4. Embrace ambiguity
5. Be optimistic
6. Collaborate
7. Take ownership

- Set aside a couple of undisturbed, meeting-free hours where you can focus without distraction.
- Clear your mind enough to be receptive to the feelings that arise when you see certain words and phrases. Ideas to do this include:
  - Meditating
  - Doodling
  - Flipping through magazines or photo albums
  - Journaling
- When you look back at the personal story mapping exercise, consider what particular words, feelings or themes emerged.
- To begin your own list, brainstorm whatever comes up for you and write it all down.
- See whether you notice any related groupings or places where there is overlap in a similar vein.
- Be more specific or add an anecdote to each that illustrates how you practice or recognize the value.
- Come up with a list of 3-6 along with a short personal observation of why each one matters to you.
- Write them down and keep them somewhere handy. They will act as your inner compass as you navigate your journey.
- Gather all of this material in one place that is accessible and easy to work with and rearrange. For example, you could use a notebook, file, or pin items to a corkboard. Think of this as a sandbox of ideas you can always return to as a key reference point.

ACTIVITY 3.3 - NOTES

Learning Outcome

Learn about tools to access inner courage or motivation through stories and metaphors.

Learning Notes

"What if we all rose to hear the call, picked up the sword, or somehow summoned something deep, primal, and fierce in ourselves to go on an epic quest?"

"Heroes identify, take a stand and fight for, liberate, and protect the important things."

"Letting go of judgment around where your skills and talents are not can be just as freeing as recognizing where they are, because it's all being done in the context of what you're amazing at. It's impossible to be great at everything."

"We cannot, and indeed should not, strive to be everything."

Learning Materials

Book:

- *The Greater Good* - Chapter 4: Picking Up the Sword
- The hero's journey or quest as a motivational metaphor for stepping into one's leadership and the desire to heal, prove, or vanquish.

Archetype Resources:

- Branding with Archetypes: *https://freerange.com/blog/branding-free-range-with-archetypes*
- Goddesses the Archetypes of Femininity: *https://www.ajourneytoyourself.com/goddesses-archetypes-femininity/*
- Paper or spreadsheet

Key Terms and Definitions

Archetypes

A set of commonly recurring, iconic character types.

Quest

An adventurous journey in search of something.

Questions for discussion

- What does it take to go from inspiration to action?
- What are some tools for identifying our unique gifts and strengths, or giving us courage to step into a new role or idea of ourselves as entrepreneurs?

Additional Resources

Book:

Archetypes in Branding: A Toolkit for Creatives and Strategists by Margaret Hartwell and Joshua C. Chen *https://www.simonandschuster.com/books/Archetypes-in-Branding/Margaret-Hartwell/9781440308185*

CHAPTER 4 - ACTIVITIES

ACTIVITY 4.1:

ARCHETYPE DISCOVERY

Learning Materials

Book:

- *The Greater Good* - Chapter 4

Archetype Resources:

- Branding with Archetypes: *https://freerange.com/blog/branding-free-range-with-archetypes*
- Goddesses the Archetypes of Femininity: *https://www.ajourneytoyourself.com/goddesses-archetypes-femininity/*

Format

Self-reflection with option for group sharing.

Archetypes are useful to us as entrepreneurs because they help us frame our own leadership style and journey. Did any figures or characters pop up for you as part of this discussion in the book or your exploration of traditional archetypes? Did anything come to mind?

- Explore the archetype resources.
- Look back at your values exercise. What matters enough that you are willing to risk something - title, money, reputation, failure - to obtain it?
- Look at the issues that inform your voting choices, political events you attend, organizations you donate to, brands you admire, or even things you would be willing to take up arms to protect.
  - What stirs you about these issues and what personal connection do you have to them?
- Who are your personal heroes and why do they inspire you?
  - What aspects of their character impress you the most?
- If you had all the power in the world at your fingertips, what would you do with it?
  - What change would you create and why?
- Start to notice whether there are patterns of behaviors, conflicts, relationships, or other aspects that persistently show up in your life.
  - What are the lessons you seem to keep relearning?
  - Are there recurring issues, dreams, dramas?
  - What won't leave you alone?
- Do you resonate with more than one archetype? There is no need to pick just one.
- You can also create your own archetype! What is your version of an archetype? If you could make up your own, what would it be?
  - Would it be based on your personal heroes or people you admire?
  - Would it be based on movies that have resonated with you or images that mean something to you?
  - Would it be based on a childhood experience?
- What is that part of you that is your truest self?

ACTIVITY 4.1 - NOTES

ACTIVITY 4.2:

GENIUS ACTIVITY

Learning Materials

Book:

- *The Greater Good* - Chapter 4

Format

Do this activity alone or with a partner who knows you well.

The Genius Quadrant Tool allows you to isolate the activities at which you uniquely excel and, ideally, will be able to invest the greatest position of your time and energy doing.

- Get a piece of paper and make 4 quadrants or columns
- Label each as:
    - **Incompetent** = No-go list
        - Stuff you either intensely dislike or are not gifted at
    - **Competent** = So-so or mediocre
        - You can do it but there are other folks who are better at these tasks than you
    - **Excellent** = Things that are easy for you, which you are skilled at, and enjoy
        - They are also skills that others likely have and may not truly light you up
    - **Genius** = The ultimate sweet spot (Note: There can be more than one.)
        - What distinguishes this list is that it's unique to you.
            - What do you bring that nobody else does?
            - What's irreplaceable about you?
            - What makes your heart sing?
- Make a thoughtful list of personal skills and attributes that they feel belong in each category.
- If you are working with someone else, compare lists and discuss.

ACTIVITY 4.2 - NOTES

CHAPTER 4 - ACTIVITIES

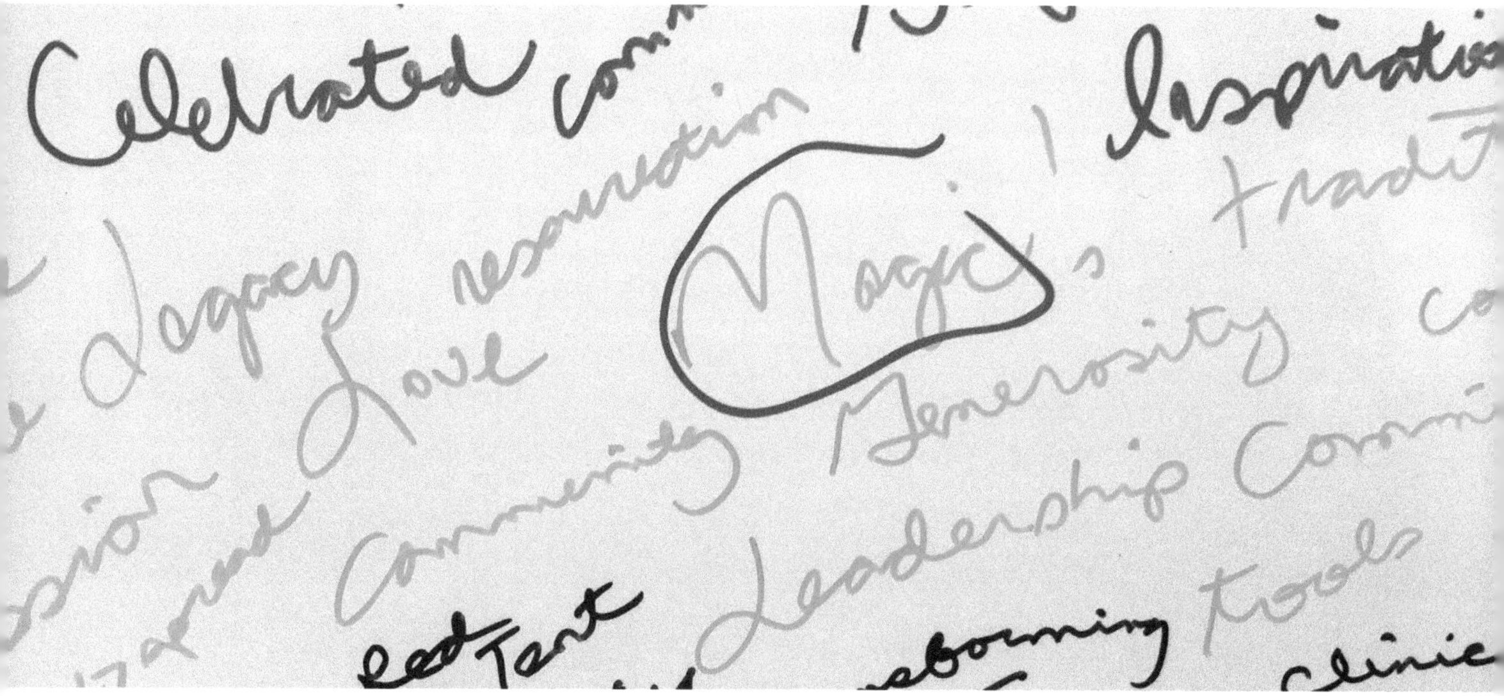

ACTIVITY 4.3:

HIDDEN SUPERPOWERS

Lesson Materials

Book:

- *The Greater Good* - Chapter 4

Format

Individual activity or work with a partner or in a small group.

Genius is a great tool for understanding skills. Hidden superpowers are about things that are less quantifiable. Discovering and sharing these can also be a powerful team building activity.

Examples shared by Madeleine:

- Having frank but gentle conversations with people about issues they are confronting in their careers or with their businesses
- Having insightful ideas, images, and questions popping into her head that are not necessarily directly related to what the person is saying
- Opening an emotional frequency for people that does not often get touched
- What are some of your sources of power that are perhaps less obvious, a bit strange, or flat-out weird?
- Consider what types of reasons people are drawn to you or the things they seek you out for.
  - Do they ask you specific questions or see comfort or counsel from you in certain situations?

ACTIVITY 4.3 - NOTES

Learning Outcome

Access and craft your vision for change on an emotional level from your lived experience, personal history, and values.

Learning Notes

"Vision is the single most compelling element of any venture."

"People involved in a project simply need to be able to see, feel, and find themselves in its vision."

Learning Materials

Reading materials:

- *The Greater Good* - Chapter 5: Exploring Vision
- How readers can uncover and nurture their vision, with inspiration from spotlighted social entrepreneurs.
- Aisle's *Are You There, God? It's Me, Margaret* Legacy *https://periodaisle.com/blogs/all/aisle-s-are-you-there-god-it-s-me-margaret-legacy*

Videos:

- How to Be a Social Entrepreneur Video Course: Episode 2: Exploring Vision (7:09) *https://www.youtube.com/watch?v=gzflBXJTYig*
- Meet Aisle (4:25) *https://vimeo.com/395043346*
- The G Day Movement (2:21) *https://www.youtube.com/watch?v=LeLmDfZ046E&t=3s*
- What is Nestworks (3:59) *https://www.youtube.com/watch?v=h_Jeu-sPOxU*

Key Terms and Definitions

Credo

A statement that would be on your personal coat of arms, or the most succinct summary of what you're bringing to your time on the planet.

Manifesto

A longer poetic style of expressing your values, vision, mission, purpose, and anything else you feel is key to your pursuit.

Mission Statement

Succinctly defines your purpose and vision.

Vision

The answer to what form of change you are trying to create and why.

Discussion Questions

- Where did Madeleine's visions come from for Lunapads, Nestworks and G Day?
- What similarities and differences can you see in terms of how they presented themselves?
- What are some tools to access and express vision?

CHAPTER 5 - ACTIVITIES

ACTIVITY 5.1:

THE SOURCE OF VISION

Learning Materials

Book:

- *The Greater Good* - Chapter 5
    - The Lunapads/Aisle Story
    - The Nestworks Story

Videos:

- How to Be a Social Entrepreneur Video Course: Episode 2: Exploring Vision (7:09) *https://www.youtube.com/watch?v=gzflBXJTYig*
- Meet Aisle (4:25) *https://vimeo.com/395043346*
- The G Day Movement (2:21) *https://www.youtube.com/watch?v=LeLmDfZ046E&t=3s*
- What is Nestworks (3:59) *https://www.youtube.com/watch?v=h_Jeu-sPOxU*

Format

Self-reflection or group discussion.

- Revisit "The Lunapads/Aisle Story" and "The Nestworks Story" in *The Greater Good*. Watch the videos listed in the learning materials.
- Where did the visions come from for Lunapads, Nestworks and G Day?
- How did Madeleine move from story to vision for each of these ventures?
- What similarities and differences can you see in terms of how they presented themselves?

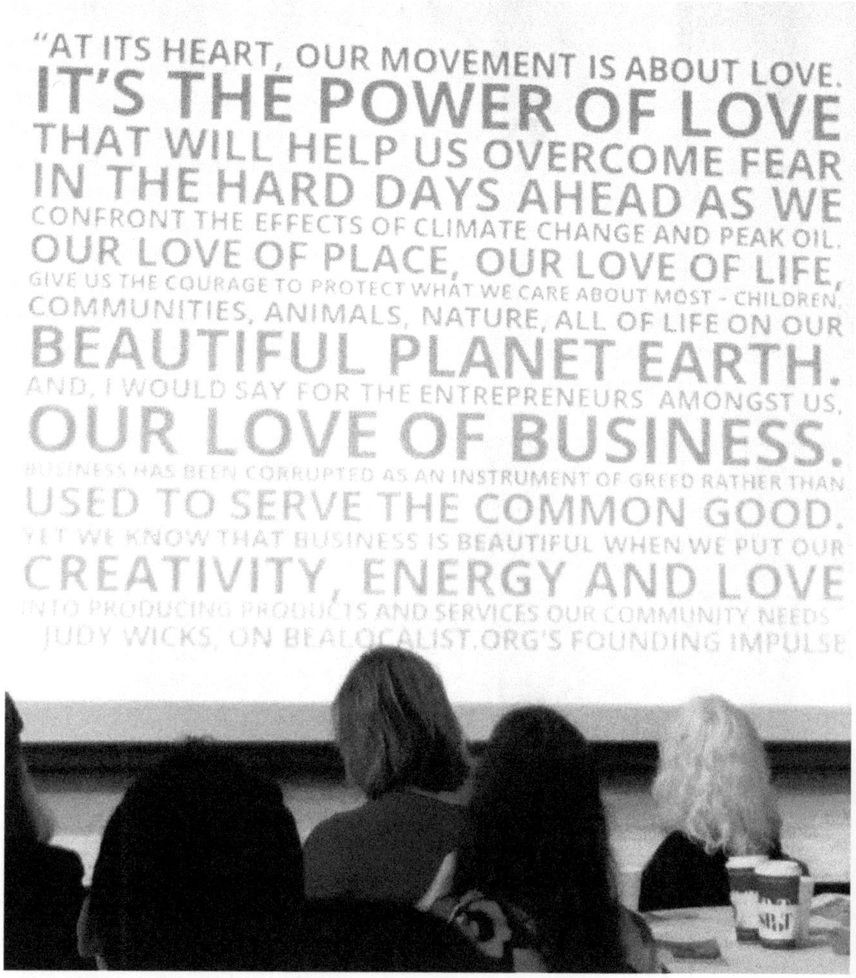

ACTIVITY 5.1 - NOTES

ACTIVITY 5.2:

VISION QUEST

Learning Materials

Book:

- *The Greater Good* - Chapter 5

Format

Self-reflection with option for group sharing.

A vision quest involves intentionally taking time out of your regular routine to open yourself up to receiving or going deeper with your vision. Do whatever it takes to get out of your head, reflect on ideas or feelings that you may have pushed aside, or otherwise enter a different mental state outside of what is normal for you. Take note of what comes up for you.

General tips for a mini vision quest:

- Spend time in nature
- Look at or make art
- Look at old photographs
- Read old journals, blog posts, letters, or other pieces of writing you have created
- Do something unusual for you; try something different (e.g. language/music class, exercise, meditation, drawing, writing with your non-dominant hand)
- Explore a part of your community where you don't normally spend time
- Go away somewhere with the intention of letting go of old ideas and being intentionally open to new ones
- Write a letter to your future self
- Play games
- As you do these things, record whatever it is you are seeing and feeling. What's happening? Words, feelings, or images that came up? What's happening physically in your body?
- Create a voice recording on your phone/tablet, or make a quick video
- Draw a picture or create a mind map of what you're seeing and feeling. Indicate any relationships between images or words and let it be messy
- Tell someone about what you experienced and invite them to ask questions to tease out details
- Add anything you create to the work you may have already done. Are there any patterns emerging?
- Notice how it feels in your body
- Freewrite by hand about whatever is coming up for you
- Look at images in old magazines and intuitively arrange them; notice what words and images attract you
- Visit a domain registry and search URLs that come to mind

CHAPTER 5 - ACTIVITIES

What if you don't have a vision yet?

- Consider what it was that drew you to the concept of social entrepreneurship in the first place?
  - Which words got your attention? What hope or other feeling did you have about the concept we refer to above? This feeling is a potential key.
- Perhaps you know someone whose vision you're drawn to. Describe what attracts you to it and how you see yourself supporting it.
- Remain curious
- Write things down
- Turn them over in your mind
- Pay particular attention to events, conversations, and random things that pique your interest

ACTIVITY 5.2 - NOTES

ACTIVITY 5.3:

DETECTIVE EXERCISE

Lesson Materials

Book:

- *The Greater Good* - Chapter 5

Format

Individual exercise with option for group sharing.

Detectives look for clues in unexpected places. You are looking for something that does not yet exist (at least, not your version of it). Acting like a detective is another way to uncover, summon, or otherwise access your vision.

- Keep a scrapbook
  - Newspaper articles, photographs, postcards, business cards, notice when something stays with you or keeps coming into your mind (conversation, phrase)
- If you see something similar to what you want to create, find out as much as you can about it.
  - Informational interviews, Googling, rearranging information and images into new patterns, discussing ideas with others (may lead to introductions and connections to others with expertise and support)
- Share your ideas liberally and ask for help
- Check in regularly with how you are feeling
- Pay close attention to what you say
  - What do you notice? What words or phrases do you use frequently? What stories do you commonly tell? Do you notice any patterns?

ACTIVITY 5.3 - NOTES

ACTIVITY 5.4:

INNER CHILD MEDITATION EXERCISE

Learning Materials

Book:

- *The Greater Good* - Chapter 5

Format

Self-reflection or a small group feedback session with trusted friends and/or colleagues.

An inner child meditation is a regression meditation, through which you discover what your younger self has to tell you. It involves taking time to revisit your former self and to find out what your inner child or youth has to say. It provides great insight into things you may have forgotten, or become distracted from. Consider getting a small group of trusted friends and colleagues together for a personal feedback session.

Option 1: Personal reflection

- Set aside an hour or so at at time when you are feeling grounded and know you won't be interrupted
- Take it slowly and see what comes up
- Inner child meditation suggestions (p. 67 - 68 in *The Greater Good*)

Option 2: Small group feedback session

Consider getting a small group of trusted friends and colleagues together for a personal feedback session.

- Ask them what gifts and talents they see in you.
    - There may be something that surfaces that you don't perceive in yourself, but others do.

ACTIVITY 5.4 - NOTES

ACTIVITY 5.5:

ARTICULATING YOUR VISION

Learning Materials

Book:

- *The Greater Good* - Chapter 5

Format

Individual exercise with option for group sharing.

However you end up exploring your vision, come up with a way to articulate it.

- This could be something visual, a short (5-10 words) list, a poem, a statement (e.g. a mission statement), a credo, or a manifesto.
- Keep in mind that this will be refined as you move along in your journey.
- You don't need to do all of these! Pick one or two that feel right for you.

Here are examples of a mission statement, credo, and manifesto:

- A mission statement succinctly defines your purpose and vision
    - Example: Lunapads' first mission statement:
        - *To create more positive and informed relationships between women, their bodies and the Earth.*
- A credo is a statement that would be on your personal coat of arms, or the most succinct summary of what you're bringing to your time on the planet.
    - Example: Coralus's credo:

      We practice Radical Generosity, which we believe is core to creating a new and better world.

      We have all that we need in this network to reach our potential.

      If you need something, ask.

      If you have something to give, please offer it.

      We are all at different stages and ages and we come from different experiences.

      We are here with our sleeves rolled up, ready to help one another.

      This is a co-created environment built on trust.

      We are creating a space for women to thrive on their own terms.

      We take our time, and we consider the future.

      We celebrate and embolden each other.

      We amplify each other's voices.
      We own our greatness.
- A manifesto is a longer poetic style of expressing your values, vision, mission, purpose, and anything else you feel is key to your pursuit

- Example: CreativeMornings manifesto:

  Everyone is creative.

  A creative life requires bravery and action, honesty and hard work. We are here to support you, celebrate with you, and encourage you to make the things you love.

  We believe in the power of community. We believe in giving a damn.
  We believe in face-to-face connections, in learning from others, in hugs and high fives.

  We bring together people who are driven by passion and purpose, confident that they will inspire one another, and inspire change in neighborhoods and cities around the world.

  Everyone is welcome.

ACTIVITY 5.5 - NOTES

Learning Outcome

Feel inspired and equipped to share your story with others in multiple situations.

Learning Notes

"Stories have the power to literally change reality from one state to another, to birth ventures and change lives."

Learning Materials

Book:

- *The Greater Good* - Chapter 6: Crafting Your Story
- How to craft, articulate, and share your story, with guidance on making presentations and asking for help.

Video:

- How to Be a Social Entrepreneur Video Course: Episode 3: Crafting Your Story (9:16) *https://www.youtube.com/watch?v=6MCFeAqyCLQ*
- Madeleine Shaw speaks at Pecha Kucha Night Vancouver Volume 26 *https://www.youtube.com/watch?v=RIXkKX54fJY*
- Video for Optional Activity: Wendy Palmer - Leadership Embodiment Centering Exercise (3:17) *https://vimeo.com/85008647*

Podcast:

- Menstrual Equity and Social Entrepreneurship *https://www.humconsulting.ca/podcast/2022/episode-46-menstrual-equity-and-social-entrepreneurship*

Key Terms and Definitions

Brand

The way a product, company, or individual is perceived by those who experience it.

Crafting a Story

Sharing your vision of your venture in a way that helps whoever hears it find their role and feel inspired to come on board.

Pitch

A shorthand oral version of your vision for your venture.

Pitch Deck

A visual presentation of your venture story.

USP

(Unique Selling Proposition or Value Proposition) - In one sentence, what makes your offering different from others.

Discussion Questions

- What role does storytelling play in developing an entrepreneurial venture?
- What are the basic elements of the venture/story that need to be addressed?
- What are some key ways to communicate one's story with others?

Optional Activity: Centering Exercise

Learning Materials

Book:

- *The Greater Good* - Chapter 6
- Video: Wendy Palmer - Leadership Embodiment Centering Exercise (3:17) *https://vimeo.com/85008647*

Format

Self-reflection exercise.

You may want to prepare yourself energetically prior to a storytelling opportunity. Centering encourages elevation and a sense of rising to an occasion. It provides the experience of your energy going up, out, and expanding outward in all directions to take up more space than you are accustomed to. Once you have completed one of the options below, imagine welcoming wherever it is you will be speaking to into your sphere.

Photo: MJ Araujo

Option 1:

1. Start by standing as tall and strong as you can, feeling your breastbone broaden. On an inhale breath, place one of your hands on the top of your head and gently compress it, then feel yourself spring up when you remove it.
2. Slowly exhale and feel your chest soften and open. Think of something that delights you or makes you smile.
3. Spread your arms out into space around you, imagining beautiful light emanating from your hands. Imagine this light as a sphere that surrounds you, taking up as much space as you feel like.
4. Settle into this energy and become aware of your surroundings.

Option 2:

A streamlined version of this is to breathe, remember your posture (think "strong spine, soft heart"), expand your personal space, think of something that delights you, and look into the space around you.

Option 3:

Watch Video: Wendy Palmer - Leadership Embodiment Centering Exercise (3:17) *https://vimeo.com/85008647*

CHAPTER 6 - ACTIVITIES

ACTIVITY 6.1:

HONING YOUR STORY IDEAS

Learning Materials

Book:

- *The Greater Good* - Chapter 6

Video:

- How to Be a Social Entrepreneur Video Course: Episode 3: Crafting Your Story (9:16) *https://www.youtube.com/watch?v=6MCFeAqyCLQ*

Format

Individual exercise with option for small group sharing and feedback.

If you're a social entrepreneur seeking support for your impact-based project or venture, it's helpful to use the word "story" as opposed to the word "pitch". We're not trying to convince someone of something. We are engaging them emotionally so that they can find themselves in our vision. Once you have established a clear vision for your venture, you are going to need to hone your idea so you can clearly articulate it to other people.

Option A:

Use a linear approach to record your ideas by answering the questions below.

Option B:

Create a mind map. Start with the beneficiary in the middle and place all related aspects of their lives around them. Draw lines connecting things that rely on, relate to, or intersect with one another.

- Whichever option you choose (A or B), think about:
  - The Why
    - What is the problem you are solving? What is the impact you are hoping to create? What are you trying to lift up, heal, or otherwise improve?
  - The What
    - What is your good, service, solution, or idea?
  - The Who
    - Who are the people involved in your vision including you, who you serve, and whoever else is on your team or otherwise supporting you (e.g. mentors, advisory board members, consultants etc.)?
  - The How
    - What is your plan for achieving your "what"?

ACTIVITY 6.1 - NOTES

CHAPTER 6 - ACTIVITIES

ACTIVITY 6.2:

TELLING YOUR STORY

Learning Materials

Book:

- *The Greater Good* - Chapter 6

Video:

- How to Be a Social Entrepreneur Video Course: Episode 3: Crafting Your Story (9:16) *https://www.youtube.com/watch?v=6MCFeAqyCLQ*
- Example slide deck: G Day *https://youtu.be/RIXkKX54fJY?si=jrwy5jgQdkBDkw_O*
- Madeleine Shaw Speaks at Pecha Kucha Night Vancouver: Women Transforming Cities. *https://youtu.be/RIXkKX54fJY*

Format

Individual exercise with option for small group sharing, collaboration, and feedback.

In articulating your idea to others you are telling your story. Your story is your calling card for your actionable vision and your credibility as a leader. The next step is to put yourself out there, whatever that means to you. You are seeking to create an emotional connection with whoever is listening. You are not trying to convince someone of something. Rather, you want them to find themselves in your vision.

Storytelling tips:

- Remember the hero's journey
- Don't overgeneralize or hyperbolize market potential for your idea
- Resist temptation to bombard people with facts and statistics
- Ask potent questions to draw your listeners into your story
- How many of you have struggled with (the pain point you are solving for) or know someone who has?
- Tell the story of where your idea came from honestly and succinctly
- Close with a specific actionable ask
- Practice on people
- Notice how you feel when you are telling your story
- Make it a conversation

Create a slide format presentation to share your story with others.

- **Name and description**
  - Include your logo, website address, and an attractive related image
- **Why = The problem you are trying to solve; the pain point you are addressing**
  - In what way do you want the world to be different?
  - What is the story behind your initiative?
  - What impact do you seek and for whose benefit?
- **Your Solution**
  - How will you fix the problem and make the world a better place?
- **What**
  - The details of your product, service, or other offering

- **Who = Your Team**
  - Advisors, mentors, and organizations who have offered to support you
  - Customers, donors, volunteers, beneficiaries
- **Industry or Segment Overview**
  - Related offerings
  - Whitespace = places where others in your field are not
  - Overview of related products, services, or organizations
  - Potential partners
- **USP (unique selling proposition or value proposition)**
  - In one sentence, what makes your offering different from others?
- **Money = Business or Revenue Model**
  - Grants, donations
  - How will your project be sustainable from a financial perspective?
- **Go to market strategy (reaching beneficiaries)**
  - How will people hear about you? How will you maintain relationships with them?
- **Resources and needs (people, money, relationships)**
  - What are your assets and what are you missing?
- **Next steps and call to action**
  - What are you going to do next and what do you want whoever is looking at this to do? How does your venture bring whoever is seeing or receiving this into your quest?
    - Social media follows, e-newsletter signups, volunteer hours, introductions, mentorship, petition signatures, donations, investment

ACTIVITY 6.2 - NOTES

ACTIVITY 6.3:

PARTNER STORY SHARING ACTIVITY

Learning Materials

Book:

- *The Greater Good* - Chapter 6

Format

Partner or small group exercise.

It is important to practice telling your story. You can practice with random people or do some role-playing with a receptive friend, colleague, or mentor as you will do in this exercise. You can pretend that your role-play partner is many different people: investor, neighbor, politician, random stranger, and so on.

- Choose a story to tell a partner or a small group:
  - Choose a story about your venture OR
  - Choose a story about something significant that happened to you that changed your life and shaped who you are today
- Share your story (about 3 minutes)
- Have your partner or other group members provide you with 1 minute of feedback:
  - How the story made them feel as a listener
  - Any advice about how the storytelling could be improved
    - How it was structured
    - Anything that might have been confusing
    - What could have been emphasized more
- Notice how you felt telling your story
  - Do you feel butterflies or feel nauseous, or calm and grounded?
  - Tune in and see what's there, rather than pushing past or trying to ignore what your body may be telling you.
  - Pay close attention to any verbal slips or turns of phrase that seem to come out of nowhere.
  - Write them down and think about them.
- Pay close attention as well to the person or people that you are speaking to, as though you are imparting something personally important to them that you may never have the opportunity to share again.
- Have your partner or other group members share their story and receive feedback as well

ACTIVITY 6.3 - NOTES

Learning Outcome

Recognize the value of human relationships, trust, authenticity, and empathy in business and learn how to build relationships and community to support your venture.

Learning Notes

"A new ethos of collaboration, collective well-being, reciprocity, regeneration, and relational thinking needs to define our practice as social entrepreneurs."

"If our goal is to support the greater good, then we need to see ourselves as colleagues and builders, not competitors."

"You will always learn something or otherwise derive benefit; even if it's only to learn about what does not work for you, when you put yourself out there."

"A lot of us are waiting for someone else to give us permission to act or approve of our idea."

"Tell everyone you know - and especially people you don't know - your ideas. They are contagious in the best possible sense."

"Relationships that are merely transactional never yield the same kind of rewards as those that are reciprocal."

"The success of your enterprise will largely be determined by the quality of relationships that you create to support it."

Learning Materials

Book:

- *The Greater Good* - Chapter 7: Relationships and Community Building
- Social entrepreneurs cannot go it alone. Dispelling the 'lone wolf' myth, this chapter explores the benefits of joining like-minded communities and organizations, seeking out mentors, and building advisory boards.

Video:

- How to Be a Social Entrepreneur Video Course: Episode 4: Relationships and Community Building (10:00) *https://www.youtube.com/watch?v=q3YRwlWkA3M*

Article:

- "Zebras Fix What Unicorns Break" (Zebras Unite, 2017): *https://medium.com/zebras-unite/zebrasfix-c467e55f9d96*

Video:

- Jesse Brown - "Looking for Zebras (not Unicorns) in Post-Disruption Creative Spaces" (5:41) *https://www.youtube.com/watch?v=VI9KdY85pNw*

What does the future hold for Canada? Are our institutions and economy at odds with rapid technological and cultural change? Are we keeping up? From business to government to media, disruption is here. Technology and media expert Jesse Brown explains the challenging shifts ahead, and how to stay on top of them.

Key Terms and Definitions

Advisory Board

A non-voting and less formal version of a corporate board of directors there to offer feedback and advice

Coach

A highly skilled individual with a primary focus on your agenda, goals, and accountability; will help you discover your own answers to your challenges and get you where you want to go

Incubator

A program that gives very early stage companies access to mentorship, investors and other support to help them get established

Mentorship

The guidance provided by a mentor, an experienced and trusted advisor, to help you grow your skills, make decisions, and gain new perspectives

Partnership

A formal agreement made by two or more parties to jointly manage and operate a venture

Social capital

The latent aggregate value of the relationship and communities that you are part of; having the ability to call on others for support; your personal "human resources"

Unicorn

A metaphor for a startup company with a billion-dollar valuation independent of revenue or profitability; the needle in a haystack of Silicon Valley venture capitalists

Zebra

A metaphor for a more abundant and realistic venture that is more colorful (as in for profit and purpose), yet does not get nearly the level of attention, or dollars, that a unicorn grabs

Discussion Questions

- What is the value for social entrepreneurs of being part of communities?
- Why do authentic relationships matter in a business context?
- Explain the Zebra vs. Unicorn model.
- What are some different ways to develop authentic relationships and join communities?

Additional Resources

Book:

According to economist Kate Raworth, the rapid growth sought by traditional ventures only occurs naturally with cancer cells. In her book, *Doughnut Economics,* she says, *Healthy hierarchy is achieved when nested symptoms serve the greatest whole of which they are a part. Liver cells serve the liver, which in turn serves the human body; if those cells start to multiply rapidly, they become a cancer, no longer serving but destroying the body on which they depend.*

- Why do you think that in traditional business education that it is valorized to grow an enterprise in a way that nothing grows naturally?

CHAPTER 7 - ACTIVITIES

ACTIVITY 7.1:

COMMUNITY MAPPING

Learning Materials

Book:

- *The Greater Good* - Chapter 7

Video:

- How to Be a Social Entrepreneur Video Course: Episode 4: Relationships and Community Building (10:00) *https://www.youtube.com/watch?v=q3YRwlWkA3M*

Format

Self-reflection with opportunity for partner or small group discussion.

Madeleine is of the firm belief that a new ethos of collaboration, collective well-being, reciprocity, regeneration, and relational thinking needs to define our practice as social entrepreneurs. She says, "In case you still think that you will be able to successfully bring your vision to life on your own, you can probably guess by now what I am going to say: forget it."

You are already a part of communities where you have trust and social capital. Social capital is the latent aggregate value of the relationship and communities that you are part of. It is your personal "human resources" and having the ability to call on others for support. It is not about using people for a sales relationship. It is understanding the dynamic of already having something and not starting from ground zero.

Reflect on these questions and/or record your thoughts and ideas on a piece of paper or on sticky notes.

- What communities are you already a part of? For example, are you part of a parenting group, a faith based group, an online community, or a sports team?
- What do you bring to these communities?
- What do you or can you gain from these communities?

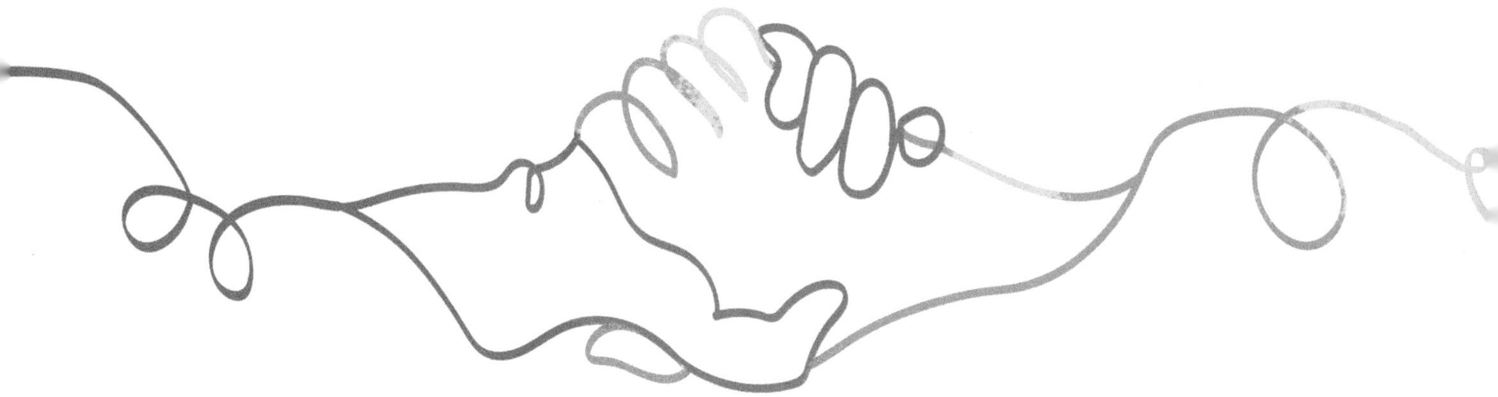

ACTIVITY 7.1 - NOTES

ACTIVITY 7.2:

ZEBRAS AND UNICORNS

Learning Materials

Book:

- *The Greater Good* - Chapter 7

Article:

- "Zebras Fix What Unicorns Break" (Zebras Unite, 2017): *https://medium.com/zebras-unite/zebrasfix-c467e55f9d96*

Video:

- Jesse Brown - "Looking for Zebras (not Unicorns) in Post-Disruption Creative Spaces" (5:41) *https://www.youtube.com/watch?v=VI9KdY85pNw*

Format

Open ended discussion with a partner or in a small group.

Why zebras?

(From the Article: "Zebras Fix What Unicorns Break" (Zebras Unite, 2017)

To state the obvious: unlike unicorns, zebras are real.

- Zebra companies are both black and white: they are profitable and improve society. They won't sacrifice one for the other.
- Zebras are also mutualistic: by banding together in groups, they protect and preserve one another. Their individual input results in stronger collective output.
- Zebra companies are built with peerless stamina and capital efficiency, as long as conditions allow them to survive.

From: *zebrasunite.coop*

Thinking critically about the concepts of zebras and unicorns:

- Were these concepts new to you?
- How do these concepts make you think about small business and enterprise in your community?
- What do they make you think about in terms of the notion of entrepreneurship?
- What is valued in a capitalist society?
- How does each perspective view growth and scale?
- What are the bigger picture implications with regards to economics and capitalism with the zebra vs unicorn paradigm?
- Think about an ecosystem. What are the implications if we had more herds of zebras vs everybody feeling like they need to be a unicorn and counting themselves out if they are not?

ACTIVITY 7.2 - NOTES

ACTIVITY 7.3:

RELATIONSHIP BUILDING STRATEGIES

Learning Materials

Book:

- *The Greater Good* - Chapter 7

Video:

- How to Be a Social Entrepreneur Video Course: Episode 4: Relationships and Community Building (10:00) *https://www.youtube.com/watch?v=q3YRwlWkA3M*

Format

Individual challenge exercise.

There are a number of different strategies that can be implemented to find the right support network, to build a community, and to have collective support around a venture.

- Joining like-minded communities
- Education and incubators
- Volunteering
- Mentorship
- Coach
- Partnerships
- Advisory boards

When you put yourself out there and actively engage and interact with others, you will always learn something or otherwise derive benefit, even if it's only to learn about what does not work for you.

Your challenge is to commit to taking a step that will help you to do this and to have telling your story be part of this in some way. This is a personal challenge so do something that will be meaningful to you, that is doable, that will move you forward, and that will take you outside of your comfort zone - even just a little bit. Nobody is checking in on you or grading you on this challenge. Ultimately, you are going to have to do this sooner or later so commit to taking on the challenge now. Be creative and playful. Choose something that aligns authentically with who you are. You've got this!

You could:

- Attend a meeting
- Go to an event
- Meet someone new and tell them your story
- Sign up with a coach
- Tell your story to a friend
- Attend a conference

CHAPTER 7 - ACTIVITIES

	Unicorn	Zebra
The Why:		
Purpose	Exponential growth	Sustainable prosperity
End game	Exit, liquidity event, 10x	Profitable, sustainable, 2x
Outcome	Monopoly	Plurality
The How:		
Worldview	Zero sum, winners and losers	Win-win
Method	Competition	Cooperation
Natural model	Parasitism	Mutualism
Resources	Hoarded	Shared
Style	Assertive	Participatory
Seeks	More	Enough, better
The Who:		
Beneficiary	Private, individuals, shareholders	Public, communities
Team composition	Engineer heavy	Balanced: Community managers, customer success, engineers
User pays	With attention (opaque)	For value (transparent)
The What:		
Growth direction	Hockey stick	Regenerative growth
Metric	Quantity	Quality
Priority	User acquisition	User success
Obstacle	Product adoption	Process adoption

Courtesy of Zebras Unite

ACTIVITY 7.3 - NOTES

Learning Outcome

Create an actionable plan to move your project forward by connecting with users, immersing yourself in their experience, and developing a product/service that meets their needs and that shows you have been listening and learning.

Learning Notes

"Get people to care on a specific, personal level and engage them in ways that are accessible, relevant, and meaningful in their lives."

"No margin, no mission."

"If your project does not make financial sense, it will be impossible to deliver on the value or change that you seek."

Learning Materials

Book:

- *The Greater Good* - Chapter 8: Bringing Your Initiative to Live
- Ways to conceive your product and build a business model, with guidance on understating your target customer and value proposition.

Business Model Canvas Resources:

Videos:

- Strategyzer: Business Model Canvas Explained (2:19) *https://www.youtube.com/watch?v=QoAOzMTLP5s*
- The Business Channel: The Business Model Canvas - 9 Steps to Creating a Successful Business Model (9:41) *https://www.youtube.com/watch?v=IP0cUBWTgpY*

Strategyzer:

- Strategyzer is a global leader in enterprise growth and innovation services.
  - The Business Model Canvas *https://www.strategyzer.com/library/the-business-model-canvas*
    - Download a PDF of The Business Model Canvas

Circulab:

- Circulab's vision is to initiate change to achieve a Circular Economy. They help businesses, entrepreneurs, cities and many more shift towards a more resilient model and design regenerative solutions.
  - Circular Canvas: Circular Business Model Template: *https://circulab.com/toolbox-circular-economy/circular-canvas-regenerative-business-models/*
    - With the Circular Canvas, you can create the outline of a business model with its various flows, and identify key impacts for users, for your region, and for the ecosystems around you.
    - With this tool, you take into account the system around the user and design a solution to meet your needs. By adopting a systemic way of thinking, you keep in mind the points to watch and can design for regeneration.

User Journey Resource:

Nesta:

- Nesta is the UK's innovation agency for social good. They design, test and scale new solutions to society's biggest problems, changing millions of lives for the better.
  - Nesta: User Journey Storyboard *https://media.nesta.org.uk/documents/prototyping_toolkit_storyboard.pdf*
    - A storyboard template to map out your user journey

Prototyping and User Testing Resources:

Nesta:

- Prototyping Framework: A Guide to Prototyping New Ideas *https://media.nesta.org.uk/documents/prototyping_framework.pdf*
  - A highly visual and comprehensive guide to prototyping.
- Prototype Testing Plan: *https://media.nesta.org.uk/documents/prototyping_toolkit_testingplan.pdf*
  - A prototype planning template

Key Terms and Definitions

Business model canvas

A map of how a venture works from an operational and financial perspective

Cost structure

An aggregate of the various types of costs, fixed and variable, variable that make up a business' overall expenses

Fixed costs

Also known as indirect costs or overhead costs; business expenses that are not dependent on the level of goods or services produced by the business

Variable costs

Costs that change as the quantity of goods and services that a business produces changes

Delivery channel

The path or network through which your product or service travels to get to the customer, donor, or beneficiary

Margin

A profit margin; how much money is left over after expenses are deducted

Marketing mix

A strategy and series of actionable marketing tactics including social media content, advertising, events, trade shows, etc.

Market strategy

How your users will learn about and be compelled to buy into your value proposition

Prototyping

Make a working model or approximation of your product, service, or initiative that can be tested

Target beneficiary

The people whose lives and circumstances you want to change by implementing your idea

User journey

The complete sum of experiences that users go through when interacting with your company and brand.

Value proposition

(Unique Selling Proposition or Value Proposition) - In one sentence, what makes your offering different from others

Discussion Questions

- What are ways to create prototypes or other approximations of goods and services that social entrepreneurs want to develop?
- What are some basic design thinking or business modeling tools?

CHAPTER 8 - ACTIVITIES

ACTIVITY 8.1:

DESIRED IMPACT, ACTIONS, AND EXPERIENCES

Learning Materials

Book:

- *The Greater Good* - Chapter 8

Format

Self-reflection with option for small group discussion and sharing.

In order to truly put your ideas and vision out into the world, you need to shape them into a concrete offering. A meaningful step you can take to move forward is to think in terms of your desired impact, actions, and experiences.

Impact:

- How will the world be different once your venture succeeds?
- What will it look and feel like?
- What are some examples of this difference?

Actions:

- What are the actions that will be taken by your users?
- What are the exact steps that need to happen in order to create the impact?
- Map these out carefully and then compare it with what you learn later on from actual users interacting with your prototype.

Experience:

- How does this all feel to the different people who will be involved on both sides of the tale?
- How will it feel to you and your team?
- What is the experience or journey that you are offering?
- What makes it special and unique?

ACTIVITY 8.1 - NOTES

ACTIVITY 8.2:

USER OR BENEFICIARY PROFILE

Learning materials

Book:

- *The Greater Good* - Chapter 8

Format

Self-reflection with option for small group discussion and sharing.

Imagine the life of your ideal user or beneficiary and what need(s) or value(s) you will provide for them. Think about their:

- Age group or life stage
- Location
- Racial, cultural, and/or ethnic profile
- Job/career/income level
- Education
- Family status
- Values and political views
- Pain points
  - What's missing for them and how can your product/service make a difference?
- Brands they like, places they shop, other ways they spend their time, money, attention

ACTIVITY 8.2 - NOTES

ACTIVITY 8.3:
USER JOURNEY

Learning Materials

Book:

- *The Greater Good* - Chapter 8

Nesta:

- User Journey Storyboard *https://media.nesta.org.uk/documents/prototyping_toolkit_storyboard.pdf*

Format

Self-reflection with option for small group discussion and sharing.

Make a visual outline that tells the story of your user's engagement with your product or service offering. Include their emotional state at any given stage. Given that you are pursuing a social change venture, being aware and tapping into people's emotions is a critical aspect of whatever you are creating.

How will they learn about your offering?

- E.g. Word of mouth, service agency, Google search, paid marketing, etc.
- How will they be feeling?
    - E.g. Curious, surprised, relieved, fed up, etc.

What steps will they take to engage with it?

- E.g. Visit your website, send a text, stop by a physical location, etc.
- How will they be feeling?
    - E.g. Skeptical, encouraged, inspired, hopeful, etc.

What happens next?

- E.g. Newsletter signup, a purchase, learning more, booking a complimentary session, downloading a free resource, etc.
- How will they be feeling?
    - Excited, anticipatory, etc.

What happens next?

- E.g. Email follow-up, phone call, video call, etc.
- How will they be feeling?
    - E.g. belonging, seen, heard, etc.

At what point is someone "converted"?

- If there is a financial transaction, what is it and when does it occur?
- If the action is, for example, dropping off donated items somewhere, where does this happen?

How will they be feeling?

- Easeful, satisfied, connected, vindicated, empowered, etc.

Follow-up: How do you acknowledge and retain the user?

- What is the quality of the relationship that you have created?
- What will keep them coming back and/or telling others?

ACTIVITY 8.3 - NOTES

ACTIVITY 8.4:

PROTOTYPING AND USER TESTING

Learning Materials

Book:

- *The Greater Good* - Chapter 8

Nesta:

- Prototyping Framework: A Guide to Prototyping New Ideas *https://media.nesta.org.uk/documents/prototyping_framework.pdf*
- Prototype Testing Plan: *https://media.nesta.org.uk/documents/prototyping_toolkit_testingplan.pdf*

Format

Individual or group exercise with opportunity for sharing ideas and feedback.

With prototyping the point is to start, learn, and iterate (AKA pivot). You will want to gather useful supplies and/or people! Role-playing can be a form of prototyping. Once you have a prototype ready, start testing it with your users.

Use the learning materials above to help you work through your prototyping and user testing. Keep notes and gather any data, questions, or feedback that show up along the way.

Prototyping

- Identify specific problems or aspects of what you are working on and document them.
- Keep an eye on how long the interactions take to make and the price of the materials.
- For services, map out the desired impact, actions, and experiences and consider how you can approximate those steps; role-playing with friends/family (community gatherings, pop up events, monthly meet-ups = experience prototypes).

User Testing

- Have a mindset that you are seeking to learn, not to prove/sell your idea.
- Having a standard survey for product testers can allow you to see common trends more easily. You may want to use anonymous surveys.
- Consider offering incentives.
- Make it fun and interesting for people to participate and give plenty of opportunities to share their needs and wants with you.
- Get help from friends and remove yourself from the proceedings if possible.
- Gather your learnings, tweak your prototype, and keep going.
- Once you have an MVP (minimum viable product), you are almost ready to go to market.
    - But first, you need to consider the financial and operational scaffolding that is going to hold everything together!

ACTIVITY 8.4 - NOTES

ACTIVITY 8.5

BUSINESS MODEL CANVAS

Learning Materials

Book:

- *The Greater Good* - Chapter 8

Business Model Canvas Resources:

Videos:

- Strategyzer: Business Model Canvas Explained (2:19) *https://www.youtube.com/watch?v=QoAOzMTLP5s*
- The Business Channel: The Business Model Canvas - 9 Steps to Creating a Successful Business Model (9:41) *https://www.youtube.com/watch?v=IP0cUBWTgpY*

Strategyzer:

- The Business Model Canvas *https://www.strategyzer.com/library/the-business-model-canvas*

Circulab:

- Circular Canvas: Circular Business Model Template: *https://circulab.com/toolbox-circular-economy/circular-canvas-regenerative-business-models/*

Format

Individual exercise with opportunity for small group discussion and feedback.

Example: Completed business model canvas for Aisle

A business model canvas metaphorically paints a picture of how your project is going to come to life. Think of a business model canvas as a living document that you can fine tune as you and your business's circumstances change. Please note that in order to obtain significant levels of funding you would need to write a more formal business plan.

Map out your social venture using the elements of a business model canvas.

Vision/Mission/Purpose/Impact statement

- The longer-term big picture, or what the world will look like when your initiative has succeeded.
- Not included in a typical business canvas.

Value proposition

- What value does your project or venture provide that would be a compelling exchange for someone's time, money, and attention?
- Keep it simple and avoid trendy business jargon.

Target beneficiary

- Also known as the individual, profile, avatar, or target customer or user.
  - Whose life are you improving?
    - What is their challenge that your offering will solve?
    - Can you share an actual story or construct a hypothetical profile based on a mix of facts and hypothesis?
    - Think about age, gender, voting tendencies, and lifestyle indicators that they might have.
    - What's their story? What else do they care about that intersects with your offering?
- Sometimes your beneficiary and your customer or donor are not the same person; be clear about this difference and make profiles for both of them.

Delivery channel

- What is the path or network through which your product or service travels to get to the customer, donor, or beneficiary? (D2C = direct to customer, wholesale channels, catalogs, consultants, dealers)

- Includes anything or anyone that your product or service goes through in order to get to the end user.

Go to market strategy

- How will your users learn about and be compelled to buy into your value proposition?
- Includes what you know about your users and the landscape.
- Includes the 4 Ps of marketing:
    - Product (or service or offering)
    - Price
    - Place (where your offering will be - store, website)
    - Promotion (marketing tactics)

Revenue and resources

- Where will the money come from (sales, grants, donations, etc.)? How is value exchanged?
- What do you need practically in order to do all of this? Do you need equipment to make your products, office space to work in, or specialized software?
- Do you need to raise capital? How much and where will it come from?

Activities

- What are the key actions to undertake to make all this work?

Partnerships and allies

- Who are these people and organizations and what role do they play? (suppliers, industry groups, other businesses and organizations, etc.)
- Make a map of these relationships and how they connect to one another

Team and leadership

- Who is on your team? (employees, volunteers, contractors, mentors, advisors, etc.)
- Think about:
    - The roles themselves in terms of title and role descriptions
    - How the roles relate to one another
- Map this out using an organizational chart

Cost structure

- What are your variable and fixed costs?

ACTIVITY 8.5 - NOTES

Learning Outcome

Develop the confidence and empowerment to understand the role money plays in social entrepreneurship and to explore ways to find funding for your venture while recognizing the importance of taking time to seek help and to heal if needed.

Learning Notes

"No margin, no mission."

"Your personal financial situation will dictate to a great extent how much time you are able to put toward your project."

"Do not, for one moment, assume that your venture will be able to support you financially in the short term."

Learning Materials

Book:

- *The Greater Good* - Chapter 9: Integration, Structure, and Funding
- How to integrate your project or venture into your life, choosing a legal structure, the social entrepreneur's relationship to money, and seeking investors and financing.

Video:

How to Be a Social Entrepreneur Video Course: Episode 5: Funding and Revenue (8:17): *https://www.youtube.com/watch?v=UMX51E56QzE*

Start-up Cost Resources:

QuickBooks:

- Article: How to Estimate Startup Costs *https://quickbooks.intuit.com/ca/resources/starting-a-business/how-to-estimate-startup-costs/*
- Video: Understanding startup costs (3:33) *https://www.youtube.com/watch?v=dt1ix3tmJJA*

Royal Bank of Canada (RBC):

- Start-up costs calculator *https://www.rbcroyalbank.com/business/pdf/Startup%20costs%20template.pdf*

Key Terms and Definitions

Cooperative

A user-owned and controlled business from which benefits are derived and distributed equally

Crowdfunding

When a group of people individually contribute funds toward a project or venture on an online platform (e.g. Kickstarter, Indiegogo, GoFundMe)

Debt

Repayable money that is typically borrowed from a financial institution as loans or lines of credit, but it can also come from other sources too, including private lenders

Donations

Non repayable money from individuals or organizations to support a specific undertaking or cause

Equity investment

Money invested in a company by purchasing shares of that company in the stock market

Financial literacy

Having the knowledge (e.g. saving, investing, debt), skills, and confidence to make responsible financial decisions

For-profit

An organization or business whose primary goal is to earn income (i.e. make a profit)

Grants

Free (non repayable) money usually given by a company, foundation, or government to an individual or a company to facilitate a goal or incentivize performance

Love money

Personal savings as well as support from friends and family

"No margin, no mission."

If a venture is not financially sustainable, you can't pay the bills or achieve the positive impact you're trying to make in the world

Nonprofit

An organization where money earned or donated is used in pursuing the organization's objectives and keeping it running

Partnership

Similar to a sole proprietorship, except there is more than one party who owns the business; a formal agreement made by two or more parties to jointly manage and operate a company

Sales

Selling your product or service to generate revenue

Sole proprietorship

Legally speaking, the business and the owner are one and the same; an unincorporated business that is owned by one individual

Start-up costs

The expenses incurred during the process of creating a new business.

Venture capital

Money, technical, or managerial expertise provided by investors to startup businesses with long-term growth potential in exchange for an equity stake

Discussion Questions

- What are different legal options for creating different types of ventures and projects?
- What role does money and financing play in a venture or project?
- What are some ways to access it, if needed?

Additional Resources

The Trauma of Money Method

- A counseling approach that addresses psychological trauma related to money *https://www.thetraumaofmoney.com*

CHAPTER 9 - ACTIVITIES

ACTIVITY 9.1:

INTEGRATING YOUR NEW VENTURE

Learning Materials

Book:

- *The Greater Good* - Chapter 9

Video:

- How to Be a Social Entrepreneur Video Course: Episode 5: Funding and Revenue (8:17): *https://www.youtube.com/watch?v=UMX51E56QzE*

Format

Individual exercise with option for small group discussion or sharing.

Achieving your vision will require resources like time and money, and access to a variety of tools that must be chosen carefully and managed responsibly. The exact quantity and quality of these resources will be dictated by the nature and scale of what you propose to undertake, as well as its legal structure. Sometimes "something's gotta give".

Your personal financial situation will dictate to a great extent how much time you are able to put toward your project, as well as if and when it takes shape as a hobby (an unpaid, volunteer passion project), side hustle (aka moonlighting, working on it alongside holding down a full-time job), or part- or full-time occupation. If you have a family or dependents, their needs will also have to be weighed as part of your choices.

Write down the following three headings or draw a three circle Venn diagram each labeled with one of the headings. Brainstorm your ideas for each one.

1. What you want to create and how much it will cost.

- How much will it cost to get your project off the ground? E.g. A website and ongoing hosting fees, branding, incorporation costs (if applicable), people's time for services like bookkeeping etc., space and equipment, materials required, labor for product assembly, marketing
- Consider the investment of your time. The value of your labor can be hard to see.

2. What resources you have to put towards creating it. Consider your funding options.

- E.g. Savings to spare? Access to family wealth? Friend or colleague contributions? Get or keep a "job job" to have the support you need until you're at a point where you can make a different choice? A partner willing and able to support you for some time?

3. What your life looks like in terms of available time to pursue it.

- Think about the full spectrum of your current commitments. Is there anything that can be put on hold, removed, or demoted from your list of main priorities?

Is there a sweet spot in the middle where you feel that you can reasonably take action, or at least make a start? Keep in mind that most initiatives take at least twice as much as we originally project.

ACTIVITY 9.1 - NOTES

ACTIVITY 9.2:

MONEY AND YOU

Learning Materials

Book:

- *The Greater Good* - Chapter 9

Video:

- How to Be a Social Entrepreneur Video Course: Episode 5: Funding and Revenue (8:17): *https://www.youtube.com/watch?v=UMX51E56QzE*

Format

Self-reflection with option for small group discussion or sharing.

Taking a personal look at what money means to you will help inform your choices and ensure they come from a healthy and realistic perspective, as you consider the financial aspects of your project. Dealing with money can be a real challenge for many of us, due to its inherent association with the for-profit world. There can be an assumption that for-profits have more money and resources than nonprofit organizations, which, especially in the case of small businesses, is often untrue.

Just in case you need to hear this, it's okay to make money (make a financial profit, pay yourself well, and build value in the equity that you own, if applicable) while you are doing something awesome for the planet and its inhabitants.

- What is your earliest memory related to money?
- What did your parents or others who raised you teach you about money?
- During your childhood, what was your family's financial reality? How were you made aware of this?
- What feelings are coming up for you as you answer these questions?
- If you are a parent, what are the main things that you want to teach your children about money?
- What's your current relationship with money like? If not one of perfect comfort, how would you like to change it?
- Do you have any role models or people you admire from a financial perspective? What makes them admirable?
- Is there an image or metaphor that you can apply to money to make it more accessible or safer, or at least more neutral?
  - Example: Madeleine thinks of money as water.
    "I now tend to think of money as water, or a form of shapeshifting, life-giving energy that can be both bad (money-laundering, greed, fraud, extortion, and blackmail come to mind) and good (freedom, generosity, abundance, pleasure, meeting unmet needs, and so on)."

ACTIVITY 9.2 - NOTES

ACTIVITY 9.3: YOUR VENTURE'S LEGAL ENTITY

Learning Materials

Book:

- *The Greater Good* - Chapter 9

Video:

- How to Be a Social Entrepreneur Video Course: Episode 5: Funding and Revenue (8:17): *https://www.youtube.com/watch?v=UMX51E56QzE*

Format

Self-reflection with option for small group discussion or sharing.

The legal form you choose should ideally be driven by your objectives, with your structure being the most effective container for them and maximizing your impact. The shape your venture takes is also related to the sources of funding and revenue that will be available to it. This would be a step where seeking professional input and advice could be valuable (business coach, lawyer, accountant).

You might not need to choose a legal entity if you are planning to create and implement a social entrepreneurship project rather than a formalized venture. It really depends on what you are trying to achieve. For example, Madeleine has been a part of projects in her community that address period poverty. Most of what their team of activists have done is garnered media attention, lobbied political leaders, and amassed and distributed donated products, costing them practically nothing.

If you do need one, what type of legal entity will house your initiative?

- **Sole proprietorship**
- **Partnership**
- **Cooperative/Co-op**
- **Nonprofit/Charity**
- **For-profit**

If you are considering the for-profit option, you may be interested in exploring for-profit values-based entities and certifications.

- Benefit corporation
- Certified B Corp

ACTIVITY 9.3 - NOTES

ACTIVITY 9.4:

YOUR START-UP COSTS AND SOURCES OF FINANCING

Learning Materials

Book:

- *The Greater Good* - Chapter 9

Video:

- How to Be a Social Entrepreneur Video Course: Episode 5: Funding and Revenue (8:17): *https://www.youtube.com/watch?v=UMX51E56QzE*

Start-up Cost Resources

QuickBooks

Article:

- How to Estimate Startup Costs *https://quickbooks.intuit.com/ca/resources/starting-a-business/how-to-estimate-startup-costs/*

Video:

- Understanding startup costs (3:33) *https://www.youtube.com/watch?v=dt1ix3tmJJA*

Royal Bank of Canada (RBC)

- Start-up costs calculator *https://www.rbcroyalbank.com/business/pdf/Startup%20costs%20template.pdf*

Format

Individual exercise with option for small group discussion or sharing.

Start-up costs:

Before you decide on your approach to funding, you need to really think about how much money you are trying to raise. What are your start-up costs? Start-up costs are the expenses incurred during the process of creating a new business. They include things such as licensing and permits, insurance, office supplies, and marketing costs. What personal resources do you have available? How quickly can you start to generate revenue?

Using the resources above, determine the start up costs for your venture.

Sources of funding:

- Love money
- Sales
- Debt
- Crowdfunding
- Grants
- Donations
- Equity investment
- Venture capital

Pick your top 3 potential sources of funding based on what you know.

- Keep in mind that the options available to you will depend on your legal entity.
- Research them. Dig deeper on the ones you have picked.
- Explore next steps to pursue them.
- What are you drawn to? What is the experience that you want to have?

ACTIVITY 9.4 - NOTES

Learning Outcome

Understand the rewards and pitfalls of the social impact space and cultivate the resilience and adaptability that will enable you to seek help, build community, embrace uncertainty, and see challenges as learning opportunities.

Learning Notes

"I can virtually guarantee you that things will not always go as planned."

"Changing the world is a practically undoable task which we are nevertheless called to do."

"If our goal is positive social change, it's radically counterproductive that it should come at the expense of anyone's well-being or mental health."

"This is my ideal reframe of what competition can look like: nobody needs to sink in order for all our boats to rise."

"There is no shame in acknowledging that we are standing on others' shoulders - the previous work that forms the foundations from which our own imaginations take off."

"There will be moments where you are going to have to take a deep breath and just make the best decision that you can with the time, information, and resources available to you."

"These are the ripples that sing as they dance between the rocks."

Learning Materials

Book:

- *The Greater Good* - Chapter 10: Facing Challenges and the Unexpected
- Ways of dealing with adversity and the unexpected, with shared stories and advice from spotlighted entrepreneurs.

Video:

- How to Be a Social Entrepreneur Video Course: Episode 6: Facing Challenges (9:00): *https://www.youtube.com/watch?v=qG-Qdpc7Wgs*

Poem:

- "Our Real Work" by Wendell Berry

Podcast:

- The Selfish Gift podcast: Madeleine Shaw, Social Entrepreneur *https://www.youtube.com/watch?v=CtlE9PgSRWs*

Key Terms and Definitions

Hustle culture

Refers to the mentality that one must work all day every day in pursuit of their professional goals

Self-doubt

Feelings of uncertainty regarding one or more aspects of the self

Unconscious beliefs

Something that we hold to be true but don't consciously think about

Discussion Questions

- What are some of the challenges that social entrepreneurs may face?
- What are some helpful ways to reframe adversity?

Additional Resources

Website:

Slow Entrepreneur Movement *https://www.slowentrepreneur.com*

- *Slow Entrepreneurship* is rooted in the belief that, as the founder of your company, your well-being is your greatest priority. When you make your well-being your top priority, you go farther, faster. We promote a set of values + practices intended to fuel your engine as you build a business that thrives.

Book:

The Emotional Entrepreneur by Scout Sobel

https://www.amazon.ca/Emotional-Entrepreneur-Scout-Sobel/dp/0578951754

CHAPTER 10 - ACTIVITIES

ACTIVITY 10.1:

A SINGING STREAM

Learning Materials

Book:

- *The Greater Good* - Chapter 10

Video:

- How to Be a Social Entrepreneur Video Course: Episode 6: Facing Challenges (9:00): *https://www.youtube.com/watch?v=qG-Qdpc7Wgs*

Poem:

- "Our Real Work" by Wendell Berry

Format

Self-reflection exercise with option for group discussion.

There is a reason we choose our seemingly irrational or unimaginable ventures, which can seem impossible to understand for those who choose a less uncertain path; and with good reason, since "changing the world" is a practically undoable task, which we are nevertheless called to. It is important that we are cultivating resilience, adaptability, persistence, creativity, and self-compassion as we grow our projects during particularly uncertain times, and that we are finding ways to see ourselves as the singing, impeded stream as we navigate our journeys.

"Our Real Work" by Wendell Berry

It may be that we we no longer know what to do
we have come to our real work,
and that when we no longer know which way to go
we have come to our real journey.
The mind that is not baffled is not employed.
The impeded stream is the one that sings.

- Think of being impeded vs. the idea of singing and being in the flow of what you are trying to create.
    - Is being impeded really a problem or is it just challenging you to find a different way to go that might be ultimately better?
- It is impossible to create a venture without experiencing challenges.
    - How do you think about challenges? In the context of the poem, what does this mean for you?
    - What are your thoughts about success vs. failure? Does a flowing stream pass or fail or is it just a stream that is flowing?

ACTIVITY 10.1 - NOTES

ACTIVITY 10.2:

RETHINKING YOUR ROCKS

Learning Materials:

Book:

- *The Greater Good* - Chapter 10

Video:

- How to Be a Social Entrepreneur Video Course: Episode 6: Facing Challenges (9:00): *https://www.youtube.com/watch?v=qG-Qdpc7Wgs*

Format:

Self-reflection with opportunity for small group discussion.

In a stream, not all "rocks" are equal. Some of them may look like obstructions but are really disguised indicators of opportunity.

"Things will not always go as planned - for better, for worse, and for weirder. As excited as you are to pursue what is calling you, there will be times of frustration, fatigue, despair, and uncertainty, and I don't just mean in terms of running your enterprise. Some of my biggest battles have been entirely internal: personal demons preying on insecurities and self-doubt. In my experience, these can have as much (or more) destructive power as a cash flow crunch or failed supplier relationship. I would also like to add that not all impediments are disastrous; some end up guiding us in unexpected ways that can be absolutely wonderful. The main thing is to let yourself begin and to maintain a sense of curiosity and flexibility about what happens next. How can you rethink or reframe the rocks that you might encounter on your venture journey? How might they initially appear to be an obstruction? How could you instead view them as an opportunity?"

Competition

- What's it like when what you thought you wanted - or who you thought you wanted to be - turns out to be different than what you had hoped for?
- Where might there be opportunities for partnership?

Your Business Model

- What happens when your business model is not working?

Self-Doubt

- What about when your challenges are internal, not external? Are your unconscious beliefs actually true? Are your expectations realistic or authentic? Do they stem from traditionally enforced social conditioning and beliefs?

Personal or Business Setbacks

- What about when things go sideways either on a personal or business level? Can you take a deep breath and just make the best decision that you can with the time, information, and resources available to you?

Change and Loss

- How can you reconcile business changes and losses that can have profoundly personal aspects? How can you use ritual as a tool for processing and providing closure?

Hustle Culture (AKA Perfectionism)

- What can you do when you are feeling stuck, stressed, or out of steam?
- Are you overloading yourself?
- Are you being gentle with yourself?
- Can you check in on your aspirations?
- Can you consider another time in your life when you met a challenge and came through it?
- Can you break what you are working on into smaller steps?
- Does it need to be done immediately?
- Can you ask for help?
- Can you find a physical way to express what you need and then create it?
- Can you have a good cry and be present with what comes up?
- Can you be of service to others?

ACTIVITY 10.2 - NOTES

Learning Outcome

Unpack the definition of success, in terms of personal sustainability and the potential of your organization, and what this means in growing and maintaining a mission-driven organization over time.

Learning Notes

"Starting an initiative that creates positive social and/or environmental impact - making the world a better place in some way, shape, or form - is the most inspiring, light-filled aspect of radiance. It's what has led you to where you are right now and inspired you to roll up your sleeves, pick up your sword, and be willing to transform. It's everything."

"When we seek to make a difference, we are, by definition, seeking to hold ourselves to a higher standard of behavior and transparency."

"Radiance, by definition, goes in all directions and can illuminate less-than-beautiful corners."

"Failure can be a learning and personal growth experience, or even something that leads the way to 'successes'."

"Who knows; perhaps you will create an alternative ending, beginning, or upcycling of your own design."

"The future is in our hands, and it needs us to be humble, proud, and brave; to trust ourselves and to relinquish the bigger-is-better, winner-takes-all values that have put us in the dubious situation in which we now find ourselves."

"It is my deepest hope that we can collectively open ourselves up to imagining, exploring, and co-creating a new, inclusive, and radiant approach to entrepreneurship - and to life, for that matter - in the name of the greater good."

Learning Materials

Book:

- *The Greater Good* - Chapter 11: Radiance
- The author's concept of radiance encapsulates impact, integrity, and endings in the social entrepreneurship space.
- "Reframing my White Woman Racism from 'Not Me' to 'Me Too'" Essay *https://medium.com/@madeleineshawgreatergood/reframing-my-white-woman-racism-from-not-me-to-me-too-b84ac957f40b*

Video:

- How to Be a Social Entrepreneur Video Course: Episode 7: Make an Impact (9:36): *https://www.youtube.com/watch?v=qrVyuBYUEho*

Anti-Oppression Resources

Website:

- Canadian Council for Refugees Power Wheel *https://ccrweb.ca/en/anti-oppression*

Article:

- "The Characteristics of White Supremacy Culture" from *Dismantling Racism: A Workbook for Social Change Groups* by Kenneth Jones and Tema Okun *https://www.whitesupremacyculture.info/uploads/4/3/5/7/43579015/okun_-_white_sup_culture_2020.pdf*
- **Updated Article: "White Supremacy Culture - Still Here" by Tema Okun, May 2021 *https://drive.google.com/file/d/1XR_7M_9qa64zZ00_JyFVTAjmjVU-uSz8/view*

Key Terms and Definitions

Allyship

Playing a conscious, supportive role to oppressed groups that one is not a member of

B Corp

A private certification of for-profit companies of their social and environmental performance

Biomimicry

The adaptation of natural systems to address complex human problems

Cooperatives

A business or other organization which is owned and run jointly by its members, who share the profits and benefits

Employee stock option plans (ESOP)

Grants employees company stock, often based on the duration of their employment

Exit to community (E2C)

Taking an organization, company, or startup where profits, decision-making, and power are held by a few and turning it into one where those same things are held by the community

Radiance

An alignment of your own integrity, the product or service you create, and how it's delivered. Multidimensional impact.

Social impact mergers and acquisitions

Traditional exit

A liquidity event; liquidating your company's assets, selling the company as a whole to another company or individual, or creating an initial public offering (IPO) on a stock market

Unconscious bias

Social stereotypes about certain groups of people that individuals form outside their own conscious awareness

Upcycling

Creative reuse; taking something old and transforming it into something new

Discussion Questions

- What does the concept of 'Radiance' mean to the author? How is it different from other more traditional metrics of success?
- What are ways for social entrepreneurs to be able to understand and measure the impact that they are having? Why is this important?

Additional Resources

Book:

- *Feminism: A Key Idea for Business and Society* by Celia V. Harquail https://www.cvharquail.com/feminism-book
- *White Women: Everything You Already Know About Your Own Racism and How to Do Better* by Regina Jackson and Saira Rao https://www.goodreads.com/book/show/60371066-white-women

Website:

- SURJ (Showing Up For Racial Justice) https://surj.org/category/resources/

CHAPTER 11 - ACTIVITIES

ACTIVITY 11.1:

SOCIAL PRIVILEGE AND IMPACT

Learning Materials

Book:

- *The Greater Good* - Chapter 11
- "Reframing my White Woman Racism from 'Not Me' to 'Me Too'" Essay *https://medium.com/@madeleineshawgreatergood/reframing-my-white-woman-racism-from-not-me-to-me-too-b84ac957f40b*
- *White Women: Everything You Already Know About Your Own Racism and How to Do Better* by Regina Jackson and Saira Rao *https://www.goodreads.com/book/show/60371066-white-women*

Video:

- How to Be a Social Entrepreneur Video Course: Episode 7: Make an Impact (9:36): *https://www.youtube.com/watch?v=qrVyuBYUEho*

Format

Self-reflection exercise with option of small group discussion.

As in all of life, when it comes to making a difference, we risk our intentions and our impact falling out of alignment with one another. For all our care and desire to help, things can go horribly wrong if we're not clear and careful, especially when there are social power imbalances present. This can appear in as many different ways as there are people and forms of oppression in the world.

If you are not a member of the population whose needs you are seeking to serve, interrogate how this distance might be shaping your perspective and assumptions. Allyship - playing a conscious, supportive role to oppressed groups that one is not a member of - is an essential part in bringing about social change; however, it requires ongoing self-awareness, clear communication, and willingness to accept and act on feedback.

Where do you have social privilege and where do you not? Write down your thoughts and ideas or draw a circle and divide it into a pie made up of 11 pieces.

Gender

Are you a cisgender man? Are you a cisgender woman? Are you trans, intersex, or non-binary?

Sexuality

Are you heterosexual? Are you lesbian, gay, queer, pan, bi, or asexual?

Ability

Are you able-bodied? Do you have health issues? Are you living with a disability?

Skin color

Are you white? Are you a person of color?

Age

Are you middle-aged? Are you a youth? Are you an elder?

Seniority

Are you an executive or considered to be senior staff? Are you junior staff? Do you have no professional position?

Anti-Oppression Resources

Website:

- Canadian Council for Refugees Power Wheel *https://ccrweb.ca/en/anti-oppression*

Article:

- "The Characteristics of White Supremacy Culture" from *Dismantling Racism: A Workbook for Social Change Groups* by Kenneth Jones and Tema Okun *https://www.whitesupremacyculture.info/uploads/4/3/5/7/43579015/okun_-_white_sup_culture_2020.pdf*
- ****Updated Article:** "White Supremacy Culture - Still Here" by Tema Okun, May 2021 *https://drive.google.com/file/d/1X-R_7M_9qa64zZ00_JyFVTAjmjVU-uSz8/view*

Experience

Do you have ample and varied experience? Are you starting out and learning the ropes?

Language

Are you English-speaking? Do you speak other languages? Are you part of the dominant linguistic culture of where you live?

Indigenous

Are you non-Indigenous? Are you Indigenous?

Formal education

Do you have a degree or formal certification? Do you have no formal education?

Citizenship

Are you a citizen? Are you a permanent resident? Are you an immigrant or refugee? Do you have precarious legal status?

Take what you have learned through this lens of social privilege and apply it to what you are trying to correct. What are you going to do with this information? How do you contextualize yourself as you engage with others? What does this mean not just for your venture but for your personal leadership as well? What is your possible disconnect between your intentions and your impact?

ACTIVITY 11.1 - NOTES

ACTIVITY 11.2:

RADIANCE AS A MEASURE OF SUCCESS

Learning Materials

Book:

- *The Greater Good* - Chapter 11

Video:

- How to Be a Social Entrepreneur Video Course: Episode 7: Make an Impact (9:36): https://www.youtube.com/watch?v=qrVyuBYUEho

Format

Self-reflection with opportunity for small group sharing or discussion.

Radiance is an alignment of your own integrity, the product you create, and how it's delivered. It is a more inclusive, organic, complex measure of success in contrast to the traditional hockey stick model with a straight diagonal line of profit/growth. Radiance is a beautiful word that implies transcendence, as well as multidimensional impact that may extend beyond your initial vision or into ripples that you never imagined.

Key aspects of radiance to consider include:

- Ways of understanding and assessing our impact
- Alternative ways of looking at endings
- Consideration of the integrity of our leadership practice as much as that of our product/service

Understanding and assessing impact:

Articulate ways that your project or venture can have value or impact beyond the traditional metrics of financial success, customer acquisition, and amount of geographical territory covered. Dig deep in terms of what impact the vision will have. Broaden your thinking about what success and impact mean and get creative with this.

- How can you bring as much value and maximize impact with what you are creating?
- How might you do this in creative and unexpected ways?
- Consider the following examples of just some of the ways that Lunapads/Aisle has made an impact. What strikes you about this list? What do you notice about it?
  - Since 2000, 200 million disposable products, and counting, have been diverted from landfills thanks to customers switching to Lunapads/Aisle products.
    - Lunapads/Aisle
      - Has made over $100,000 in cash donations to AFRIpads and is a proud shareholder in the internationally recognized, groundbreaking venture, whose products (originally inspired by Lunapads) have reached over 3.5 million girls.
      - Has directly donated over $225,000 worth of pads, cups, and underwear to communities in need throughout Canada, the Caribbean, Asia, and Africa, reaching over thirty thousand girls.

- Has collaborated with AFRIpads to co-produce a booklet about menstrual health called *Girl Talk!*. *Girl Talk!* has since been expanded into a full curriculum that has reached over thirty-two thousand NGO educators in nine countries, who have in turn educated over 110, 000 women and girls about the menstrual cycle, reproductive anatomy, and personal hygiene practices.

Integrity of leadership practice

Do a self-examination of your leadership style and aspirations and what these mean to you. Your leadership should align with the impact you seek to have. We don't want to take social impact ventures, ideas, and services and have a leadership style that takes a traditional stance. This creates misalignment.

- How do you see yourself as a leader?
- What is your leadership style?
- What do you assume about your leadership? Do you believe that you need to be the boss or are you open to a more collaborative style of leadership?
- Examine and gain clarity on what you seek to achieve personally as a leader.
- Examine the relationship you have with the entity you are creating and try to understand where they may overlap.
- What are your motives and how are they being expressed?

ACTIVITY 11.2 - NOTES

Learning Outcome

Reflect on your insights from and experience with *The Greater Good* and determine and articulate your next steps.

Learning Notes

"Like clearing out a closet, I find that making space in life often invites in what wants to happen next."

"Make peace with yourself. Avoid burnout. Consider your boundaries. Ask for support. You cannot be all things to everyone - and that's okay."

"What if everything is already perfect? What if the only thing I actually need to do right now is just breathe?"

Learning Materials

Book:

- *The Greater Good* - Chapter 12: Next Steps and Resources

What the reader will come away with after reading this book, lists extensive resources, and offers encouragement for moving forward.

Madeleine Shaw's website:

- Resources *https://madeleineshaw.ca/resources/*

Check out these awesome resources, communities, books and more that support social entrepreneurship!

Discussion Questions

- What are you committing to?
- What are you doing next?
- What might be in the way or holding you back?

CHAPTER 12 - ACTIVITIES

ACTIVITY 12.1:

YOUR NEXT STEPS

Learning Materials

Book:

- *The Greater Good* - Chapter 12

Madeleine Shaw's website:

- Resources *https://madeleineshaw.ca/resources/*

Check out these awesome resources, communities, books and more that support social entrepreneurship!

Format

Self-reflection exercise.

You may already be feeling clear on your goals and have them well underway - wonderful! Or you may still be sifting ideas, doing research and reviewing the activities discussed here. That's equally good.

A question to those of you who have not already taken action: is there something that you need to let go of in order to move forward? Contrary to some, I do not necessarily believe that you can "have it all" - or if you can, probably not all at once.

I would encourage you to continue to read, research, follow, witness, join, and otherwise take in the amazing conversations, organizations, and initiatives unfolding out there in the "blue ocean" - and online. Sooner or later, a moment of inspiration or a new relationship will show up and you'll know that it's time to get moving.

- What has your experience with *The Greater Good* changed in you? How has it inspired you?
- What are the personal insights that you are taking away from *The Greater Good*?
- Even if you aren't ready to start a venture, what are you going to do next?
- What are you committing to? What are you doing next? What might be in the way or holding you back?

Remember that it's okay if it just doesn't feel right to take action at this moment. Maybe it's time for you to rest, consider the possibility of other options, take stock, tend to other aspects of your life, or simply be still. Trust that wherever this is going that it will happen in its own time.

ACTIVITY 12.1 - NOTES

BONUS LESSON

Learning Outcome

Share your key insights and takeaways from *The Greater Good* to keep the conversation going and the ideas flowing.

Learning Materials

Book:

- *The Greater Good* - Chapter 11: Radiance

The author's concept of radiance encapsulates impact, integrity, and endings in the social entrepreneurship space.

Discussion Questions

- What are your key takeaways from the book? What are some ideas, points of inspiration, and insights that you didn't have before?
- Who are you now that you weren't before?

BONUS ACTIVITY: PARTING THOUGHTS

Learning Materials

Book:

- *The Greater Good* - Chapter 11

Format

Ongoing self-reflection and/or a small group conversation.

Let's keep the conversation going and the ideas flowing. Have a look below at the recap of the central thoughts from *The Greater Good*. You can refer to these for a quick hit of inspiration as you continue your quest. These are suggestions and things that I have learned but I encourage you to make this list your own. Listen to your venture, your mind, your heart, and your wisdom.

- What have you learned?
- What are your key takeaways from the book?
- Who are you now that you weren't before?
- What are some ideas, points of inspiration, and insights that you didn't have before?
- What would you add to this list?
  - Add your own thoughts, ideas, and examples that may have come up as you were reading *The Greater Good* or working through the learning activities in this toolkit.
  - Reach out and share your key takeaways and additions to this list at: *hello@greatergood.work*

Recap of some of the central thoughts from *The Greater Good*:

- See whatever you pursue as a deeply personal and creative form of self-expression, or even an art.
- See first to collaborate, not compete. Saving the world is not a zero-sum game. Playing by the old rules will not get us where we need to go.
- Remember Melody Biringer's wisdom: relationships are the true currency.
- Treasure your outside or "margin" qualities. Please read Arlan Hamilton's *It's About Damn Time: How to Turn Being Underestimated into Your Greatest Advantage* - especially if your experience is as a person who falls outside the dominant power paradigm.
- Be aware that you are likely conditioned toward linear forms of thought and try to start unlearning them. Ask yourself what other forms of knowing and intelligence might also be real, worthy, and available. Read adrienne maree brown's *Emergent Strategy.*
- Consider which lessons we might learn from nature as we consider models for our initiatives. Check out Kate Raworth's TED talk, "A Healthy Economy Should be Designed to Thrive, Not Grow", as well as Melanie Rieback's TED talk, "Post-Growth Entrepreneurship."

- Honor transitions with care and intention. There is power in ritual that can literally work magic and transform our efforts into the quest they really are.
- Reframe transactional thinking as relational thinking. Cherish the human moments at times that just feel like paperwork.
- Be attuned and open to diverse, creative ways of understanding agency, partnership, and planning. Think collectively, rather than individually.
- Cultivate a possibility mindset. What if the regular rules didn't apply? What if you could set your own terms?
- Do not take positive impact as a given; be mindful, self-aware, and diligent.
- Consider the principle of equitable design; how might this be relevant to your product, service, or initiative?
- Consider how your initiative can support widespread, progressive systems change, not just its own (or your) success.
- Ask yourself whether there is an opportunity to level up your initiative from "good" to "greater" by infusing values into the How, not just the What and Why.
- Think beyond existing or traditional concepts of scale and success.
- Lift as you rise. Respect and make room for others, especially if you carry social privilege.
- No margin, no mission.
- Move gracefully and nurture things.
- Stay in your corner.
- Be the singing stream.
- Practice radiance.

BONUS ACTIVITY - NOTES

Milton Keynes UK
Ingram Content Group UK Ltd.
UKHW050634010424
440413UK00006B/103

9 781738 174706